ELAINE LOMBARDI

The G.I.F.T.S. Method

The Five Keys System to Lasting Change

MEL BOOKS

Contents

Dedication

For my amazing children—Kristina, Andrew, Daniel, and Joseph
Every good thing I've learned about life,
I learned while being your mom.
Thank you for filling my world with love, light, and laughter.
You grew up hearing me say, "Attitude is so Important!"
This book carries that same truth onto the page: the attitude
you bring to your growth changes what's possible in your life.
To watch you become the incredible adults you've become
is the greatest reward of my life. I write this book hoping to support
the next steps of your beautiful journeys.

G.I.F.T.S. Core Manual

The G.I.F.T.S. Method: The Five Keys System to Lasting Change is the core manual for the G.I.F.T.S. framework. It introduces the five key areas—Gratitude, Intuitive Intention, Family & Friends, Treasured Wisdom, and Self-Love & Care—and shows you how to integrate them into one coherent way of living.

WARNING: This book is designed for **doing, not just reading**. Reading this book straight through will feel repetitive. That's intentional. **This is an implementation program, not a book to read in one sitting.** Each chapter is meant to be read, practiced for days or weeks, then the next chapter begun. Information consumption over integration is the exact problem this book addresses. Please follow the How to Use This Book section to get the most out of this book.

All other G.I.F.T.S. books, journals, and resources are designed to complement this manual by exploring specific stories, themes, and applications of the G.I.F.T.S. method.

HOW TO USE THIS BOOK

This is not a book to read—it's a system to practice.

If you read straight through for information, you'll find repetition. That's by design. Each chapter builds on practices you should be implementing before moving forward.

The right way to use this book:

- Read Chapters 1-3 to understand the framework
- Read Chapter 4 (Gratitude) and practice for 3-7 days
- Read Chapter 5 (Intuition) and add those practices while maintaining gratitude. Continue this pattern through all five keys
- Use the 30-Day Integration System as your implementation guide
- Reference the Daily Practice Guide throughout

Why this matters: Information consumption over integration is the exact problem this book addresses. Reading about transformation is not transformation. The "repetition" you'll notice if you read straight through serves as retrieval practice for those actually implementing the work.

You have a choice:

- Read it like every other self-help book (and get the same results).
- Use it as the systematic implementation program it's designed to be and get the results you deserve.

The knowing-doing gap exists because people collect insights instead of living them. Don't let this become another book on your shelf.

G.I.F.T.S. Method Roadmap

Use this as your at-a-glance roadmap. Return to it whenever you need to remember what each chapter is helping you practice. Always keep in mind: *change comes from implementation, not information.*

The Stack of Good Intentions

- You are not broken or undisciplined; repeated false starts come from missing systems and identity-level integration.
- The G.I.F.T.S. method turns five key areas into one integrated way of being, so change feels natural.

The Knowing–Doing Gap

- Insight alone does not create change; automatic patterns run the show until they are retrained through experience.
- Smart, self-aware people often suffer more because understanding becomes a substitute for action.

Hidden Cost of Inspiration Without Implementation

- Inspiration without follow-through erodes self-trust, fuels cynicism, and creates quiet shame around growth.
- Seeing past attempts as system failures, not character flaws, is key to rebuilding hope.

Why Willpower Always Fails

- Willpower is a limited daily resource, so relying on it guarantees relapse under stress.
- Habit-stacking, environmental design, and identity-based change make desired behaviors automatic.

The Integration Principle

- Gratitude, intuition, relationships, wisdom, and self-love are expressions of one integrated way of being.
- Working all five together creates a positive feedback loop where progress in one area amplifies the others.

Beginning the Implementation Process

- Start by naming three knowing–doing gaps without judgment, then take one tiny action in each G.I.F.T.S. area today.
- Make small environmental tweaks and reset your inner narrative with a compassionate letter to yourself.

The Integrated G.I.F.T.S. Method

- The five keys quiety shape your emotional state, resilience, and fulfillment.
- Weakness in one key can undermine everything; strengthening all five builds a stable foundation.

Why These Five Keys Matter

- Gratitude sets your lens; intuition shapes decisions; relationships give meaning and safety.
- Treasured wisdom turns life into learning, and self-love and care supply

the energy to sustain change.

Your Roadmap (Five Phases)

- Change moves through phases: build practices, integrate and face resistance, become automatic, deepen, then live as your integrated self.
- Milestones and troubleshooting help you know what to expect and how to keep going.

The Implementation Infrastructure

- Structural, psychological, and social supports make follow-through easier than giving up.
- The system is designed to lighten over time so it never becomes another heavy "self-improvement job."

When Life Gets Messy (Recovery)

- Lapses are expected; what matters is how quickly and kindly you return, not perfection.
- Recovery questions turn setbacks into learning instead of evidence of failure.

The Ripple Effect – Changing Patterns

- Every relationship is a system; when you change, the system must reorganize.
- Staying steady, kind, and boundaried allows relationships to reset around healthier patterns.

The Ripple Effect – Inspiring Change Without Being Preachy

- Modeling is more powerful than fixing; people trust what they see you live.
- Share practices when asked and lead with empathy and curiosity instead of unsolicited advice.

Deepening Your Practice – Ready to Go Deeper

- Advanced practice begins when the basics feel natural, flexible, and principle-driven.
- Signs of readiness include gratitude for challenges and comfort with uncertainty.

Deepening – Advanced Implementation

- The work shifts from self-fix to service; G.I.F.T.S. becomes a lifestyle that benefits others.
- Practices evolve from checklists into fluid, responsive ways of living your values.

Deepening – Intuitive Leadership from Inner Wisdom

- Intuitive leadership integrates inner knowing with wise analysis for major decisions.
- Your calm, grounded choices naturally draw others to seek your perspective.

Deepening – Creating Your G.I.F.T.S. Legacy

- Legacy is who you are, not what you preach; your presence and choices model integrated living.
- Capturing and sharing your wisdom extends your influence.

1

THE STACK OF GOOD INTENTIONS

The stack of personal development books on your nightstand tells a story you know by heart. Each one promised to be different, to finally bridge that gap between understanding what would make your life better and actually living that way. You bought them with genuine hope, read the first few chapters with real excitement, maybe even started implementing some strategies for a week or two. Then life happened, old patterns crept back in, and another book joined the collection of good intentions.

You're not broken. You're not lacking willpower or discipline. The problem runs much deeper than individual motivation, and the solution requires a completely different approach than anything you've tried before.

Most personal development resources operate on the assumption that you need more information, better strategies, or stronger inspiration to create change. This assumption creates a fundamental mismatch between what you actually need and what you're being offered.

You already know gratitude matters. You understand that listening to your intuition would lead to better decisions. You recognize that your relationships with family and friends need more attention and care. You've collected wisdom from dozens of sources, and you're aware that treating yourself with compassion would improve everything. The knowledge isn't missing. The system for consistently applying that knowledge is what's missing.

This book operates on a radically different premise. Instead of giving you more things to know, it gives you a way to live what you already know. Instead of inspiring you to change, it provides the infrastructure for change to happen automatically. Instead of asking you to remember five new habits, it shows you how to integrate five interconnected key areas of life until they become who you are rather than what you do.

All my life, I've come back to one simple truth that I repeated to my children over and over: *"Attitude is so important!"* At the time, I meant it as a reminder that we can't always control what happens, but we can always choose how we meet it on the inside. In many ways, this book is the grown-up, fully developed version of that same message about building a way of living where your inner attitude to gratitude, intuition, relationships, treasured wisdom, and self-love quietly reshapes everything else.

The G.I.F.T.S. method stands for Gratitude, Intuitive intention, Family and Friends, Treasured Wisdom, and Self-love and Care. These five key areas represent the foundation of human fulfillment, but more importantly, they support and strengthen each other in ways that create sustainable transformation. When you develop gratitude as a natural response rather than a forced practice, it opens your heart to receive intuitive guidance more clearly. When you trust your intuition, you make better decisions about how to show up for the people you love. When your relationships are nourished, you feel safer to apply the wisdom you've gathered and treat yourself with the care you deserve.

This interconnected approach solves the problem that has derailed your previous attempts at change. You've been trying to fix one area at a time, which requires enormous willpower and creates internal conflict. Your mind resists isolated changes because they don't align with your overall way of being. But when you work with all five key areas simultaneously, each one reinforces the others and change begins to feel natural rather than forced.

Why This Is Different

Every failed attempt at personal transformation follows the same predictable pattern. You encounter an idea that resonates deeply, maybe through a book, workshop, or conversation with a friend who seems to have figured something out. The idea makes perfect sense, and you can immediately see how applying it would improve your life. You feel motivated, maybe even excited, and you start implementing the new approach with genuine commitment.

For a few days or weeks, things go well. You practice gratitude each morning, or you start paying attention to your gut feelings, or you make more effort to connect with your family. You notice positive changes and feel hopeful that this time will be different. Then something shifts. The new behavior starts feeling forced rather than natural. Other priorities demand your attention. The initial motivation fades, and you find yourself back in familiar patterns.

You blame yourself for lacking discipline or consistency, but the real problem lies in how change actually works versus how you've been taught to pursue it. The real turning point is not just having a better plan; it's the attitude you bring to that plan.

When you approach change with an attitude of curiosity instead of criticism, patience instead of panic, and willingness instead of perfectionism, your brain and nervous system stop treating transformation as a threat. That's what I meant all those years when I told my kids, "Attitude is so important!" The way you meet your own growth, from the inside out, determines whether new practices become part of who you are or just another short-lived experiment.

Most personal development approaches treat transformation like a collection of separate improvements. They ask you to add gratitude practices to your morning routine, develop better intuition through meditation, improve your relationships through better communication, apply wisdom through journaling, and practice self-care through various activities. Each of these suggestions makes sense individually, but they create an impossible burden. You're essentially trying to become five different people at once, and your existing identity fights back against this fragmentation.

Your subconscious mind, which governs most of your daily behavior, rejects changes that don't fit with your overall sense of who you are. This creates internal resistance that feels like laziness or lack of motivation, but it's actually your psychological immune system protecting you from what it perceives as threats to your coherent sense of self.

The G.I.F.T.S. method works differently because it recognizes that lasting change happens at the identity level, not the behavior level. Instead of asking you to do five new things, it helps you become someone who naturally embodies gratitude, trusts intuitive guidance, nurtures relationships, applies wisdom, and treats yourself with care. This shift from doing to being eliminates the internal conflict that has sabotaged your previous efforts.

The method also addresses the sustainability problem that plagues most personal development approaches. When you rely on motivation or willpower to maintain new behaviors, you're drawing from a limited resource that gets depleted by stress, fatigue, and competing demands. But when new behaviors emerge from an integrated identity, they become automatic responses that don't require conscious effort to maintain.

You've probably experienced glimpses of this automatic quality in other areas of your life. If you're a parent, you don't have to remember to care about your children's wellbeing. It's built into who you are. If you're good at your job, many of your professional skills operate without conscious thought. The G.I.F.T.S. method extends this same automatic quality to the areas of life that matter most for your overall fulfillment and growth.

The integration happens through specific daily practices that connect all five key areas rather than treating them as separate projects. When you practice gratitude in the morning, you're not just checking off a self-improvement task, you're opening your heart to receive clearer intuitive guidance throughout the day. When you follow that guidance, you naturally make better choices about how to show up for the people you love. When your relationships are nourished, you feel more secure and open to applying the wisdom you've gathered. When you apply that wisdom consistently, you naturally treat yourself with greater care and compassion. This creates an upward spiral where progress in one area automatically supports progress in all the others.

Instead of fighting against your existing patterns, you're working with the natural tendency of integrated systems to reinforce themselves. The result is transformation that feels sustainable because it's not being imposed from the outside, it's emerging from a new way of being.

The Fundamental Shift

Something I call the implementation infrastructure represents the fundamental shift in how personal development works. Instead of hoping you'll follow through on good intentions, this system ensures that you actually do something with what you learn. The infrastructure operates on three levels: structural, psychological, and social. Each level addresses a different reason why previous attempts at change have failed, and together they create conditions where sustainable transformation becomes inevitable rather than hopeful.

The structural level provides the framework that makes consistent action easier than inconsistent action. Most people fail to maintain new behaviors because their environment and schedule aren't designed to support them. You might want to practice gratitude each morning, but if you don't have a specific time, place, and method for doing it, the practice depends entirely on remembering and feeling motivated. The G.I.F.T.S. method eliminates this dependency by building new behaviors into existing routines and creating environmental cues that prompt the actions you want to take.

For gratitude, this means identifying a specific moment in your existing morning routine where gratitude practice fits naturally, such as right after you pour your first cup of coffee or while you're waiting for your computer to start up at work. You'll have a simple, repeatable format for the practice that takes less than two minutes and connects directly to something you're already doing. This removes the friction that typically prevents new habits from sticking.

The same structural approach applies to all five key areas. Intuitive intention gets built into your decision-making process through specific questions you ask yourself before making choices, both small and significant. Family and friends connection happens through weekly practices that get scheduled like appointments and monthly practices that get added to your calendar. Treasured wisdom gets applied through a simple system for capturing insights and a weekly review process that ensures you actually use what you learn. Self-love and care gets integrated into daily transitions and evening routines.

The psychological level addresses the internal resistance that emerges when you try to change. Your mind will generate doubts, excuses, and distractions that can derail even the best-designed systems. The implementation infrastructure includes specific protocols for working with this resistance instead of fighting against it. You'll learn to recognize the early warning signs that you're starting to drift away from your practices, and you'll have concrete steps to take that get you back on track without self-judgment or starting over.

This psychological component includes what I call the recovery protocol: a systematic approach to getting back into your practices after you've missed a few days or weeks. Most people abandon their efforts entirely when they break their streak, but the recovery protocol treats these lapses as normal parts of the change process rather than failures. You'll have specific actions to take on the day you notice you've been off track, specific ways to ease back into your practices without overwhelming yourself, and specific methods for learning from the lapse so it's less likely to happen again.

The social level recognizes that lasting change rarely happens in isolation. You need support, accountability, and connection with others who understand what you're trying to accomplish. The implementation infrastructure includes guidance for creating this social support, whether through existing relationships or new connections. You'll learn how to talk to your family about the changes you're making in ways that invite their support rather than their skepticism. You'll discover how to find or create a community of people who are also working on integrating these five key areas into their lives.

The social component also includes accountability structures that don't depend on other people being available when you need them. You'll have methods for checking in with yourself weekly and monthly, tracking systems that show you patterns in your behavior over time, and celebration practices that acknowledge your progress in ways that motivate continued effort.

What makes this infrastructure different from the accountability systems you might have tried before is that it's designed around your real life rather than an idealized version of how you think you should live. It assumes you'll have busy weeks, stressful periods, and competing priorities. It assumes you'll sometimes forget, sometimes resist, and sometimes doubt whether any of this is worth the effort. Instead of treating these challenges as obstacles to overcome, the system treats them as predictable elements to work with.

The infrastructure also evolves with you as the practices become more natural. In the beginning, you'll need more structure and reminders. After a few months, the practices will require less conscious effort and the support systems can become less intensive. After six months to a year, many of the behaviors will feel automatic and you'll need the system primarily for continued growth rather than basic maintenance.

This evolutionary approach prevents the common problem of outgrowing your support system. Many people start with elaborate tracking and accountability methods that work well initially but become burdensome as the behaviors become more natural. The G.I.F.T.S. implementation infrastructure includes guidance for simplifying and adapting your approach as you progress, so the system continues to serve you rather than becoming another obligation to maintain.

Your Roadmap

You've had moments where you catch a glimpse of who you could be. Maybe it happened during a quiet morning when you felt genuinely grateful for your life, or during a conversation when you trusted your instincts and said exactly the right thing, or during an evening with your family when everyone was relaxed and connected. In these moments, you experience a version of yourself that feels more authentic, more peaceful, and more alive than your usual daily experience.

These glimpses aren't accidents or temporary highs. They're previews of your integrated self. They show you what becomes possible when all five key areas of the G.I.F.T.S. method are working together naturally. The roadmap in this book is designed to make these glimpses your normal experience rather than rare exceptions.

The journey from glimpses to integration happens through five distinct but overlapping phases. The first phase focuses on establishing the basic practices in each area and learning to recognize when you're on track versus when you're drifting. This phase typically takes four to six weeks and requires the most conscious effort because you're building new neural pathways and overriding established patterns.

During this first phase, you'll start each day with a simple gratitude practice that takes less than two minutes but creates a foundation of appreciation that influences how you interpret everything else that happens. You'll begin asking yourself specific questions before making decisions, questions designed to help you access and trust your intuitive guidance. You'll implement weekly practices for connecting more meaningfully with the people you care about, and you'll establish a simple system for capturing and applying insights from books, conversations, and experiences.

The self-love and care component gets integrated through small acts of kindness toward yourself throughout the day, such as choosing the kinder interpretation of someone else's behavior, speaking to yourself the way you would speak to a good friend, and making choices that honor your needs rather than ignoring them. These practices might feel awkward or forced initially, but they're building the foundation for everything else.

The second phase, which typically begins around week six and continues through month three, focuses on integration and refinement. The individual practices start to connect with each other more naturally, and you begin to experience the synergistic effects that make the G.I.F.T.S. method so powerful. Your gratitude practice makes you more receptive to intuitive guidance. Following your intuition leads to better decisions about relationships. Stronger relationships give you more confidence to apply wisdom and treat yourself well.

During this phase, you'll also encounter and work through the deeper resistance that emerges when real change starts to happen. Your old identity will push back against the new patterns, sometimes through increased stress, relationship conflicts, or internal doubts about whether you're becoming someone your friends and family will still recognize. The roadmap includes specific guidance for navigating these challenges without abandoning your progress.

The third phase, from months three to six, is where the practices become increasingly automatic and you start to experience sustained periods of living from your integrated self rather than just glimpsing it. The morning gratitude practice becomes a natural part of waking up rather than something you have to remember to do. Checking in with your intuition before making decisions becomes as automatic as looking both ways before crossing the street. Connecting meaningfully with family and friends becomes your default approach rather than something you have to consciously choose.

This is also the phase where you'll notice that other people start responding to you differently. Your family might comment that you seem more present or more peaceful. Friends might start coming to you for advice because they sense that you've developed a different quality of wisdom. Colleagues might notice that you make decisions with more confidence and less second-guessing. These external changes reflect the internal integration that's been developing.

The fourth phase, from months six to twelve, focuses on deepening and expanding what you've established. The basic practices are now natural, so you can explore more advanced applications of each area. Your gratitude practice might expand to include appreciation for challenges and difficulties, not just obvious blessings. Your intuitive guidance might become more subtle and sophisticated, helping you navigate complex situations with greater skill.

Your relationships might deepen as you become more comfortable with vulnerability and authentic communication. Your ability to apply wisdom might expand beyond personal situations to professional and community contexts. Your self-love and care might evolve from basic kindness to genuine self-advocacy and boundary-setting when needed.

The fifth phase represents the ongoing evolution that continues for the rest of your life. The five key areas of G.I.F.T.S. become so integrated into who you are that maintaining them requires minimal conscious effort, freeing up mental and emotional energy for continued growth and contribution to others. You become someone who naturally lives from gratitude, trusts intuitive guidance, nurtures relationships, applies wisdom, and treats yourself with care.

This final phase is where you realize that the G.I.F.T.S. method has accomplished something more significant than behavior change. It has facilitated a fundamental shift in your identity. You're no longer someone who tries to practice gratitude; you're someone who sees life through grateful eyes. You're no longer someone who hopes to trust their intuition; you're someone who naturally consults their inner voice. You're no longer someone who wants better relationships; you're someone who creates connection wherever you go.

The roadmap includes specific milestones and checkpoints for each phase, so you can track your progress and know when you're ready to move to the next level. It also includes troubleshooting guidance for the most common challenges that arise at each stage, from initial resistance and forgetfulness to the more subtle forms of self-sabotage that can emerge when you're on the verge of real transformation.

Most importantly, the roadmap is designed to be flexible enough to work with your unique circumstances, personality, and life situation while being structured enough to ensure that you make consistent progress. The core lesson that underlies everything in this book is that sustainable change happens through systems, not willpower. This book provides the system. Your commitment to following it provides the energy that makes transformation inevitable rather than hopeful.

2

THE KNOWING-DOING GAP

You sit in your car after another workshop, another webinar, another conversation with a coach who promised this time would be different. The notebook beside you contains pages of insights that felt revolutionary just hours ago. You can see exactly how implementing these ideas would transform your relationships, your decision-making, your entire approach to life. The clarity is so sharp it almost hurts.

Three weeks later, that same notebook sits buried under a stack of bills and grocery lists. The insights that seemed so powerful have faded into background noise, competing with deadlines and daily obligations that feel more urgent than personal growth. You're back to the same patterns, the same reactions, the same frustrated version of yourself that showed up to that workshop hoping for change.

This cycle has repeated so many times you've lost count. Each failure feels more personal than the last, as if your inability to bridge the gap between knowing and doing reveals some fundamental flaw in your character. You start to wonder if you're just not the type of person who changes, despite the evidence that you desperately want to.

The truth cuts deeper than simple disappointment. Every day you don't live according to what you know is right, you drift further from the person you glimpsed during those moments of clarity. Your relationships operate on autopilot instead of genuine connection. Your decisions get made through anxiety and overthinking instead of trusted intuition. Your daily experience lacks the gratitude, intention, and self-compassion you know would make everything better.

Intelligence makes what researchers call "the knowing-doing gap" more painful, not less. This gap: the distance between understanding what would improve your life and actually doing it, widens the smarter you get. You can analyze your patterns with sophisticated insight, understand the psychological mechanisms behind your behavior, and articulate exactly what needs to change. This analytical ability becomes a trap when you assume that understanding should automatically lead to different actions.

Your rational mind operates like a brilliant consultant who can diagnose problems and recommend solutions with impressive accuracy. It recognizes that practicing gratitude would shift your perspective from scarcity to abundance. It understands that trusting your intuition would lead to better decisions than endless pro-and-con lists. It knows that prioritizing family connections would create more fulfillment than checking email for the fifteenth time today.

But knowing these things intellectually is completely different from integrating them into your automatic responses. Your habitual patterns operate from a much deeper level than conscious thought, controlled by neural networks that have been strengthened through years of repetition. These networks don't care about your insights or intentions. They simply execute the programs that have been most frequently reinforced.

When you try to change through willpower alone, you're essentially asking your conscious mind to override these deeply embedded programs every single time a relevant situation arises. This works temporarily when your motivation is high and your stress levels are manageable. But the moment you get tired, overwhelmed, or distracted, the old programs take over automatically.

Smart people often make this problem worse by creating elaborate systems that require constant conscious management. You might design a complex morning routine that includes gratitude journaling, meditation for intuitive development, relationship planning, wisdom review, and self-care activities.

The routine looks perfect on paper and might even work for a few weeks when you're excited about the new approach.

The system fails because it treats your conscious mind like a reliable manager who will show up every day with the same energy and focus. In reality, your conscious mind is more like a part-time employee who sometimes calls in sick, occasionally shows up late, and often gets distracted by more urgent tasks. Building sustainable change on the foundation of conscious management guarantees eventual failure.

The patterns you hate persist because they serve important psychological functions, even when they create obvious problems. Checking your phone constantly might feel compulsive and disconnected, but it also provides a sense of control and connection to the wider world. Overthinking decisions might create anxiety and delay, but it also protects you from the vulnerability of trusting your gut and potentially being wrong.

Staying busy with work and obligations might leave little time for family connection, but it also provides a clear sense of productivity and accomplishment that feels safer than the uncertain territory of emotional intimacy. Collecting insights from books and workshops might substitute for actually applying wisdom, but it also gives you the satisfaction of learning without the risk of failing at implementation.

These patterns developed as intelligent responses to past circumstances, even if they no longer serve your current situation. Your analytical mind can recognize that the patterns are outdated, but your deeper psychological systems continue operating from the original programming until they're given compelling reasons to change.

The most effective way to change these deep patterns is not through force or willpower, but through creating new experiences that demonstrate better ways of meeting the same underlying needs. When you practice gratitude consistently, your nervous system learns that appreciation provides a more sustainable sense of abundance than constant striving. When you trust your intuition and get positive results, your decision-making system updates to include your inner voice as a reliable source of guidance.

This experiential learning happens slowly and requires patience with the process of gradual integration. Your smart, analytical mind wants to speed up the timeline and control the outcome, but sustainable change operates according to biological and psychological rhythms that can't be rushed through clever strategies or intense effort.

The key is designing practices that work with your deeper systems instead of fighting against them. Instead of trying to remember to be grateful, you create environmental cues that prompt appreciation naturally. Instead of forcing yourself to trust your intuition, you start with small, low-risk situations where you can practice tuning into inner guidance without major consequences.

This approach requires a fundamental shift in how you think about change. Instead of seeing yourself as a problem to be solved through better strategies, you start seeing yourself as a complex system that can be gently guided toward more fulfilling patterns through consistent, well-designed experiences.

The Hidden Cost of Inspiration Without Implementation

Each time you get inspired without following through, something important dies inside you. Not dramatically or obviously, but quietly and progressively. Your relationship with your own potential becomes increasingly strained as the gap between what you know is possible and what you actually experience grows wider.

The first few times you failed to implement insights that excited you, the disappointment felt manageable. You blamed external circumstances, poor timing, or insufficient planning. You told yourself that the next opportunity would be different, that you'd be more prepared or have better conditions for change. This optimistic interpretation protected your sense of agency and kept hope alive.

But after dozens of cycles where inspiration faded into familiar patterns, the interpretation shifts. You start to suspect that the problem is not situational but personal. Maybe you lack the discipline that other people seem to possess naturally. Maybe you're just not the type of person who follows through on good intentions. Maybe you're destined to be a consumer of wisdom rather than someone who actually lives wisely.

These conclusions feel logical given the evidence, but they create a vicious cycle that makes future success less likely. When you approach new insights with the expectation that you probably won't follow through, you unconsciously sabotage your own efforts. You don't create the environmental supports that would make implementation easier because part of you doesn't believe you'll use them. You don't ask for help or accountability because you're embarrassed about your track record of starting and stopping.

The cynicism that develops from repeated failed attempts serves as psychological armor against further disappointment. If you don't get too excited about new possibilities, you won't be as devastated when they don't materialize. This protective strategy makes sense emotionally, but it also blocks the enthusiasm and hope that fuel sustainable change.

You begin to approach personal development content differently, consuming it more for entertainment or intellectual stimulation than for actual application. You might read books about gratitude while remaining chronically focused on what's missing from your life. You might attend workshops about intuitive decision-making while continuing to make choices based primarily on fear and overthinking.

This consumption without implementation creates a strange form of expertise where you can discuss concepts fluently without embodying them practically. You become someone who knows all the right answers but continues living according to patterns that contradict your stated values. The disconnect between your knowledge and your experience becomes a source of internal shame that you rarely discuss with others.

The hidden cost extends beyond personal disappointment into your relationships and overall life trajectory. When you consistently fail to live according to your deeper values, you lose trust in your own word. This erosion of self-trust affects every area of your life, making you more hesitant to make commitments, more likely to second-guess your decisions, and less confident in your ability to create positive change.

Your family and friends might notice this pattern even when you don't discuss it directly. They see you get excited about new approaches and then quietly abandon them weeks later. Over time, they might become skeptical about your latest insights or discoveries, not because they don't want you to grow, but because they've learned not to expect lasting changes from your periodic bursts of enthusiasm.

This external skepticism reinforces your internal doubts and creates additional pressure that makes implementation even more difficult. You feel like you have to prove yourself to people who have learned to be cautious about believing in your ability to change. The weight of their unexpressed doubt combines with your own self-criticism to create an environment where sustainable transformation feels nearly impossible.

The cost also shows up in your daily emotional experience. When you know that gratitude would shift your perspective but continue focusing on problems and complaints, you live with constant low-level frustration about your own behavior. When you recognize that trusting your intuition would reduce anxiety but continue overthinking every decision, you experience ongoing tension between what you know and what you do.

This internal conflict consumes enormous amounts of mental and emotional energy that could be directed toward creative projects, meaningful relationships, or simple enjoyment of life. Instead of feeling aligned and integrated, you feel fragmented and at war with yourself. The very insights that were supposed to improve your life become sources of additional stress because they highlight the gap between your potential and your reality.

The most insidious cost is how inspiration without implementation changes your relationship with growth itself. What should be an exciting, life-giving process becomes associated with disappointment and self-criticism. You start to avoid books, workshops, or conversations that might inspire you because you've learned to associate inspiration with eventual failure.

This avoidance cuts you off from sources of wisdom and support that could actually help, creating a downward spiral where you become increasingly isolated from the very resources you need to break the pattern. You might tell yourself that you're being realistic or protecting yourself from false hope, but you're actually reinforcing the belief that you're incapable of sustained positive change.

Breaking this cycle requires a completely different approach to implementation. One that assumes you'll encounter resistance and builds systems to work with that resistance instead of fighting against it. It also requires rebuilding trust in your own capacity for change through small, consistent successes rather than dramatic transformations that depend on sustained willpower.

Why Willpower Always Fails

Willpower operates like a muscle that gets fatigued with use, but most people treat it like an unlimited resource that should be available whenever they need it. You wake up in the morning with a certain amount of mental energy for making decisions and resisting impulses, and every choice throughout the day depletes this resource slightly. By evening, your capacity for willpower is significantly reduced, which explains why you can start the day with strong intentions to practice gratitude and end it scrolling social media instead of connecting with family.

The depletion happens faster when you're stressed, tired, hungry, or dealing with competing demands on your attention. These conditions describe most people's daily experience, which means relying on willpower for sustainable change is like trying to run a marathon while holding your breath. You might make it for a short distance, but eventually your body's limitations will override your conscious intentions.

Willpower also fails because it requires you to fight against your existing neural pathways every time you want to behave differently. Your brain has spent years optimizing for efficiency by automating responses to common situations. When your phone buzzes, you automatically reach for it. When someone asks how you're doing, you automatically say "fine" without checking in with yourself. When you face a decision, you automatically start analyzing pros and cons instead of consulting your intuition.

These automatic responses happen faster than conscious thought and feel completely natural because they've been reinforced thousands of times. Using willpower to override them is like trying to dam a river with your bare hands. You might succeed temporarily, but the water will eventually find a way around your resistance.

The solution is not stronger willpower but smarter systems that work with your brain's natural tendency toward automation instead of fighting against it. Instead of trying to remember to practice gratitude through conscious effort, you attach the practice to an existing habit that already happens automatically, like drinking your first cup of coffee or starting your car in the morning.

This approach, called habit stacking, leverages the neural pathways you've already established instead of trying to create entirely new ones through willpower. After a few weeks of consistent pairing, thinking about gratitude becomes as automatic as reaching for your coffee cup. The new behavior gets integrated into your existing routine without requiring ongoing conscious management.

The same principle applies to all five key areas of the G.I.F.T.S. method. Instead of trying to remember to check in with your intuition through willpower, you create specific decision points where pausing to sense your inner guidance becomes the automatic next step. Instead of forcing yourself to connect with family through conscious effort, you establish weekly practices that get scheduled like any other important appointment.

Environmental design plays a crucial role in making positive behaviors automatic. Your physical and digital environments are constantly cueing certain behaviors while making others more difficult. If your phone is the first thing you see when you wake up, you're likely to start the day with reactive scrolling instead of intentional gratitude. If your journal is buried in a drawer, you're less likely to capture and apply wisdom from your daily experiences.

Changing your environment to support the behaviors you want requires minimal ongoing willpower because the cues do most of the work for you. When you put your journal next to your coffee maker, you're reminded to write without having to remember. When you put your phone in another room during family dinner, you're not tempted to check it without having to resist the urge.

The most effective environmental changes are small and specific rather than dramatic and comprehensive. Moving your journal six inches to a more visible location will have more impact than buying an elaborate new planning system that requires daily maintenance. Putting a sticky note on your bathroom mirror asking "What does my intuition say about today?" will be more sustainable than committing to twenty minutes of morning meditation.

Social environment matters as much as physical environment for creating automatic positive behaviors. When you surround yourself with people who naturally embody gratitude, intuitive decision-making, strong relationships, applied wisdom, and self-care, these qualities become more automatic in your own life through unconscious modeling and social reinforcement.

This doesn't mean you need to abandon friends who don't share your values, but it does mean being intentional about spending time with people who demonstrate the qualities you want to develop. You might join a book club focused on personal growth, attend community events that attract thoughtful people, or simply have more regular contact with friends and family members who bring out your best qualities.

Identity-based change represents the deepest level of sustainable transformation because it shifts the foundation from which all your behaviors emerge. Instead of trying to act like someone who practices gratitude, you gradually become someone who sees life through grateful eyes. Instead of forcing yourself to trust your intuition, you develop into someone who naturally consults inner voice before making decisions.

This identity shift happens through consistent small actions that reinforce a new self-concept rather than dramatic changes that require sustained willpower. Each time you choose to appreciate something instead of complaining, you strengthen the neural pathways associated with being a grateful person. Each time you pause to sense your gut feeling before deciding, you reinforce your identity as someone who trusts inner guidance.

The key is focusing on the type of person you want to become rather than the specific outcomes you want to achieve. Instead of setting a goal to practice gratitude for thirty days, you commit to becoming someone who naturally appreciates life. Instead of trying to improve your relationships through better communication techniques, you focus on becoming someone who creates connection wherever you go.

This identity-based approach works because it aligns your conscious intentions with your deeper psychological systems. Your brain wants to maintain consistency between your self-concept and your behaviors, so when you genuinely see yourself as a grateful, intuitive, connected, wise, and self-caring person, acting in accordance with these qualities feels natural rather than forced.

The Integration Principle

Most personal development approaches treat different areas of life like separate projects that can be improved independently. You work on gratitude through morning practices, develop intuition through meditation, strengthen relationships through communication skills, apply wisdom through journaling, and practice self-care through various activities. Each area gets its own set of strategies, its own timeline for improvement, and its own measures of success.

This compartmentalized approach creates several problems that explain why so many well-intentioned efforts fail to produce lasting change. First, it requires you to manage multiple separate improvement projects simultaneously, which quickly overwhelms your capacity for sustained attention and effort. Second, it ignores the natural interconnections between different areas of life, missing opportunities for synergistic growth where progress in one area automatically supports progress in others.

The integration principle recognizes that gratitude, intuitive intention, family and friends connection, treasured wisdom, and self-love and care are not separate aspects of a fulfilling life, they are different expressions of the same underlying way of being. When you truly embody any one of these qualities, it naturally strengthens your capacity for all the others.

Genuine gratitude opens your heart in ways that make you more receptive to intuitive guidance. When you appreciate what you already have instead of constantly focusing on what's missing, your nervous system relaxes into a state of receptivity where subtle inner signals become more noticeable. The anxiety and mental noise that typically obscure intuitive guidance quiet down when you're genuinely grateful for your current circumstances.

Trusting your intuition leads to better decisions about how to show up in your relationships. Your gut feelings often contain important information about what the people you love actually need from you, beyond what they explicitly request or what you think you should provide. When you follow intuitive prompts to call a friend who's been on your mind, or to have a difficult conversation that you've been avoiding, your relationships deepen in ways that wouldn't happen through conscious relationship management alone.

Strong, authentic relationships create the emotional safety that allows you to apply wisdom more boldly in your life. When you feel genuinely supported and loved, you're more willing to take risks based on what you've learned, whether that means making a career change, setting boundaries, or pursuing creative projects.

Applying wisdom consistently builds the self-respect and confidence that makes authentic self-care feel natural rather than selfish. When you regularly act on what you know to be true, you develop trust in your own judgment and worthiness that translates into treating yourself with greater kindness and consideration. Self-care stops feeling like an indulgence you need to justify and starts feeling like an obvious expression of valuing yourself appropriately.

Self-love and care create the emotional stability and inner resources that support all the other areas. When you treat yourself with compassion and meet your own needs consistently, you approach life from a place of fullness rather than depletion. This makes it easier to feel genuinely grateful, to trust your inner guidance, to show up generously for others, and to apply wisdom even when it requires short-term discomfort.

These interconnections mean that working on all five key areas simultaneously is actually easier than trying to improve them one at a time. Instead of depleting your willpower across multiple separate projects, you're reinforcing a single integrated way of being that expresses itself through different channels. Progress in any area automatically supports progress in all the others, creating an upward spiral of positive change.

The integration happens through daily practices that connect multiple areas rather than treating them as separate activities. Your morning gratitude practice includes appreciation for your intuitive guidance, your relationships, the wisdom you've gained, and your own growth and healing. When you check in with your intuition before making decisions, you also consider how your choice will affect the people you love and whether it aligns with the wisdom you've collected.

Weekly relationship practices include gratitude for the people in your life, intuitive attention to what each relationship needs, communicating by sharing the wisdom you've learned, and self-care boundaries that allow you to show up sustainably. Wisdom includes grateful appreciation for insights you've received, intuitive discernment about which concepts to focus on, consideration of how implementation will affect your relationships, and self-compassionate patience with the learning process.

This integrated approach also prevents the common problem of spiritual bypassing, where people use personal development practices to avoid dealing with practical life challenges. When gratitude is integrated with intuitive decision-making and relationship attention, it becomes a foundation for engaged living rather than a way to feel better about circumstances you're not willing to change.

When intuitive development is connected to applying wisdom and self-care, it leads to grounded action rather than abstract insights that don't translate into real-world improvement. When relationship focus is balanced with self-love and applying wisdom, it creates healthy interdependence rather than codependent people-pleasing.

The integration principle also explains why previous attempts at change may have felt forced or unsustainable. When you try to add gratitude practices to a life that's still driven primarily by anxiety and scarcity thinking, the practices feel artificial and require constant effort to maintain. When you try to trust your intuition while continuing to treat yourself harshly and maintain relationships based on obligation rather than genuine connection, inner guidance becomes clouded by conflicting emotional signals.

But when you work with all five key areas as expressions of a single integrated way of being, each practice feels like a natural extension of the others. Gratitude flows easily when you're treating yourself with care and surrounded by authentic relationships. Intuitive guidance becomes clear when your heart is open through appreciation and your nervous system is calm through self-care. Relationships deepen naturally when you're approaching them from a place of gratitude, inner wisdom, and self-respect.

The result is transformation that feels organic rather than imposed, sustainable rather than effortful, and comprehensive rather than limited to one area of life. Instead of becoming someone who practices five separate self-improvement techniques, you become someone who naturally lives from an integrated place of appreciation, wisdom, connection, and self-love.

Beginning the Implementation Process

The knowing-doing gap exists because you've been approaching change from the wrong level. Your conscious mind understands what would improve your life, but sustainable transformation happens at the level of identity and automatic response patterns, not conscious intention and willpower. Every failed attempt to bridge this gap through motivation and discipline has actually reinforced the belief that you're someone who doesn't follow through, creating a vicious cycle that makes future success less likely.

The solution requires shifting from willpower-based change to systems-based change, and from isolated improvement projects to integrated development of all five G.I.F.T.S. key areas simultaneously. When gratitude, intuitive intention, family and friends connection, treasured wisdom, and self-love and care are developed as expressions of a single way of being, they reinforce each other and create sustainable transformation that feels natural rather than forced.

Your first implementation step is to identify your personal knowing-doing gaps without judgment or self-criticism. Take fifteen minutes to write down three specific examples where you clearly understand what would improve your life but consistently fail to take action. For each example, note what you know you should do, how long you've known it, and what typically prevents you from following through.

Look for patterns in your responses that reveal the deeper dynamics keeping you stuck. Do you tend to abandon practices when they start feeling routine? Do you give up after missing a few days and conclude that you've failed completely? Do you create elaborate systems that require more maintenance than the behaviors themselves? Do you avoid asking for support because you're embarrassed about your track record?

Your second step is to choose one small action from each of the five G.I.F.T.S. key areas that you can implement immediately without requiring significant changes to your schedule or environment. For gratitude, this might be appreciating one thing you can see from wherever you're sitting right now. For intuitive intention, this might be pausing to notice what your gut says about a small decision you need to make today.

For family and friends connection, this might be sending a brief message to someone you care about, telling them specifically what you appreciate about them. For treasured wisdom, this might be identifying one insight from this chapter that you can apply in the next twenty-four hours. For self-love and care, this might be speaking to yourself about a recent mistake the way you would speak to a good friend who made the same error.

Complete all five actions before moving on to the next chapter. The goal is not to create perfect practices but to experience the integration principle directly by working with all five key areas in a short period of time. Notice how each action affects your capacity for the others, and pay attention to any resistance or skepticism that arises.

Your third step is to identify the environmental and social factors that have supported your knowing-doing gaps in the past. Look around your physical space and notice what cues automatic behaviors that don't align with your values. Consider your daily routines and identify moments where you consistently choose reactive patterns over intentional responses. Think about the people in your life and notice who reinforces your identity as someone who doesn't follow through versus who supports your growth.

Write down three specific environmental changes you could make in the next week that would make positive behaviors easier and negative patterns more difficult. These should be small, concrete modifications like moving your phone to a different location, putting a journal next to your coffee maker, or scheduling a weekly call with someone who brings out your best qualities.

Your final step for this chapter is to begin shifting your internal narrative about past failures. Instead of viewing previous attempts at change as evidence of personal inadequacy, practice seeing them as valuable data about what doesn't work. Each failed diet, abandoned meditation practice, or neglected relationship goal taught you something important about the conditions you need for sustainable change.

Write a brief letter to yourself from the perspective of someone who understands that your past struggles with implementation were system failures, not character flaws. Acknowledge the courage it took to keep trying despite repeated disappointments, and express confidence in your ability to create lasting change when you have the right approach. This letter will serve as a foundation for the identity-based transformation that begins in the next chapter.

3

THE INTEGRATED G.I.F.T.S. METHOD

The integrated framework for the G.I.F.T.S. method you're about to learn represents years of testing what actually works versus what sounds good in theory. Every element has been refined through real-world application by people who share your exact frustrations with the knowing-doing gap. The G.I.F.T.S. method succeeds where other approaches fail because it treats transformation as an integrated system rather than a collection of separate practices.

Most people approach personal development like they're trying to fix a broken machine by replacing individual parts. They work on gratitude for a few weeks, then switch to improving relationships, then focus on trusting their intuition, treating each area as an independent project with its own timeline and success metrics. This approach fails because human beings are not machines with replaceable components. We are interconnected systems where every element influences every other element.

The G.I.F.T.S.method recognizes these natural interconnections and leverages them to create change that feels effortless rather than forced. When you develop genuine gratitude, it automatically opens your heart to receive clearer intuitive guidance. When you trust that guidance, it naturally leads to better decisions about how to show up for the people you love. When your relationships are nourished, you feel safer to apply the wisdom you've gathered and treat yourself with the care you deserve.

This creates what systems theorists call a positive feedback loop, where progress in any area amplifies progress in all other areas. Instead of depleting your willpower across multiple separate improvement projects, you're building momentum that makes each subsequent change easier than the last. The framework provides the structure that turns this theoretical possibility into practical reality.

Why These Five Key Areas Control Your Experiences

Your daily emotional state and overall life satisfaction are determined by five key fundamental factors that operate below the level of conscious awareness. Gratitude shapes how you interpret everything that happens to you, determining whether you experience life as abundant or scarce, meaningful or random, supportive or threatening. This interpretive lens affects every other aspect of your experience because it determines the emotional foundation from which you approach relationships, decisions, and challenges.

When gratitude operates automatically in your life, you notice opportunities instead of obstacles, appreciate progress instead of focusing on what's still missing, and feel resourced enough to be generous with others. When gratitude is absent or forced, you experience chronic dissatisfaction that no external achievement can resolve, leading to the hollow success that characterizes so many high-achieving people who feel fundamentally unfulfilled despite obvious accomplishments.

Intuitive intention determines the quality of every decision you make, from small daily choices to major life transitions. Your rational mind can analyze options and predict likely outcomes, but it cannot access the deeper wisdom that emerges from your complete life experience, your unconscious pattern recognition, and your authentic values. When you consistently override or ignore this inner guidance, you make decisions that look good on paper but feel wrong in your body, leading to a life that appears successful from the outside while feeling disconnected and inauthentic from the inside.

The quality of your relationships with family and friends creates the emotional context within which everything else in your life unfolds. Strong, authentic connections provide the safety and support that allow you to take risks, pursue growth, and recover from failures. They also provide meaning and joy that make daily challenges feel worthwhile rather than overwhelming. When these relationships are neglected or superficial, even significant achievements feel empty because there's no one who truly knows and celebrates who you're becoming.

Weak relationships also create a vicious cycle where isolation leads to poor decision-making, which leads to outcomes that create more isolation. Without trusted people to provide perspective and feedback, you're more likely to stay stuck in patterns that don't serve you, make decisions based on fear rather than wisdom, and miss opportunities for growth that would be obvious to someone who knows you well.

Treasured wisdom determines whether your life experiences contribute to your growth and effectiveness or simply accumulate as unprocessed events. Every book you read, conversation you have, and challenge you face contains insights that could improve how you navigate future situations. But without systems for capturing, reflecting on, and implementing these insights, they remain intellectual concepts rather than practical tools that actually change how you live.

People who consistently apply wisdom from their experiences develop what researchers call crystallized intelligence: the ability to draw on accumulated knowledge to solve new problems and make better decisions. This creates compound growth where each year of life makes you more effective and fulfilled rather than just older. Without this application process, you repeat the same mistakes and face the same challenges repeatedly, leading to the frustrating sense that you're not learning or growing despite having many experiences.

Self-love and care create the internal foundation that supports everything else. When you treat yourself with genuine compassion and consistently meet your own needs, you approach life from a place of fullness rather than depletion. This makes it easier to feel grateful for what you have, to trust your inner guidance, to show up generously for others, and to apply wisdom even when it requires short-term discomfort or uncertainty.

Self-neglect creates the opposite dynamic, where you approach life from a place of scarcity and exhaustion that makes every other positive quality more difficult to access. It's nearly impossible to feel genuinely grateful when you're chronically tired, to trust your intuition when you're overwhelmed by unmet needs, or to nurture relationships when you're running on empty. Self-care is not selfish indulgence; it's the foundation that makes sustainable contribution to others possible.

These five key areas also determine your resilience in the face of challenges and setbacks. When all five are strong, you have multiple resources to draw on during difficult periods. Gratitude helps you find meaning and opportunity in adversity. Intuitive guidance helps you navigate uncertainty with confidence. Strong relationships provide support and perspective. Applied wisdom helps you learn from difficulties rather than just enduring them. Self-care ensures you have the energy and emotional stability to implement solutions rather than just surviving problems.

When any of these areas is weak, your overall resilience suffers disproportionately. A person with strong relationships but no self-care becomes a martyr who burns out helping others. Someone with great self-care but weak relationships becomes isolated and self-absorbed. A person who applies wisdom but ignores their intuition becomes overly analytical and disconnected from their authentic desires. The framework succeeds because it develops all five key areas as an integrated foundation for a fulfilling life.

The Interconnection Effect

The interconnection effect represents the most powerful aspect of the G.I.F.T.S. method and the primary reason it succeeds where other approaches fail. When you understand and leverage these natural connections, working on your personal development becomes like pushing a boulder downhill rather than uphill. Each positive change creates momentum that makes the next change easier, until transformation begins to feel inevitable rather than effortful.

Gratitude serves as the foundation that makes all other positive qualities more accessible. When you genuinely appreciate what you already have, your nervous system shifts out of scarcity-driven survival mode and into a state of receptive awareness. This physiological change is measurable. Your heart rate variability improves, your cortisol levels decrease, and your prefrontal cortex becomes more active while your amygdala calms down.

These biological shifts create the optimal conditions for accessing intuitive guidance. The mental noise and emotional reactivity that typically obscure subtle inner signals quiet down when you're in a state of appreciation. Your gut feelings become more noticeable, your sense of what feels right or wrong becomes clearer, and your ability to distinguish between fear-based reactions and wisdom-based responses improves dramatically.

This enhanced intuitive capacity leads to better decisions about your relationships. Instead of operating from obligation, guilt, or social expectations, you start responding to the actual needs and dynamics present in each relationship. You might intuitively sense that a friend needs encouragement rather than advice, or that your teenager needs space rather than conversation, or that your partner needs appreciation rather than problem-solving. These intuitive responses create deeper connection and trust than any communication technique could achieve.

Stronger relationships create the emotional safety that allows you to apply wisdom more boldly in your life. When you feel genuinely supported and accepted, you're more willing to take risks based on what you've learned, whether that means having difficult conversations, making career changes, or pursuing creative projects. The fear of judgment or rejection that often prevents applying your wisdom, diminishes when you're surrounded by people who encourage your growth.

Applied wisdom builds the self-respect and confidence that makes authentic self-care feel natural rather than selfish. When you regularly act on what you know to be true, you develop trust in your own judgment and worthiness. This translates into treating yourself with greater kindness and consideration. Self-care stops feeling like an indulgence you need to justify and starts feeling like an obvious expression of valuing yourself appropriately.

Self-love and care complete the circle by creating the emotional stability and inner resources that support deeper gratitude. When your basic needs are met and you're treating yourself with compassion, appreciation becomes a natural response rather than a forced practice. You're not trying to feel grateful to compensate for self-neglect or to convince yourself that your circumstances are acceptable when they're not. Instead, gratitude emerges from a genuine recognition of the goodness present in your life.

The interconnections also work in reverse, which explains why trying to fix one area while neglecting the others rarely produces lasting results. If you practice gratitude techniques while continuing to ignore your intuition, override your needs, and maintain superficial relationships, the gratitude feels forced and unsustainable. Your deeper systems recognize the incongruence and resist the practice as inauthentic.

Similarly, if you try to develop intuitive decision-making while remaining chronically ungrateful, isolated from meaningful relationships, and harsh toward yourself, your inner guidance becomes clouded by emotional noise and unmet needs. The signals you receive will be distorted by scarcity thinking, loneliness, and self-criticism, making it difficult to distinguish between genuine wisdom and psychological reactivity.

The framework leverages positive interconnections while preventing negative ones through specific daily and weekly practices that address all five key areas consistently. Your morning routine includes gratitude that opens your heart, intention-setting that engages your intuition, and self-care that ensures you start the day from a place of fullness. Your weekly practices include relationship activities that apply your wisdom while honoring your needs and appreciating the people you love.

This integrated approach also prevents the spiritual bypassing that occurs when people use personal development practices to avoid dealing with practical life challenges. Gratitude without relationship attention can become a way to avoid addressing problems with family and friends. Intuitive development without applying wisdom can become escapism that doesn't translate into real-world improvement. Self-care without relationship consideration can become narcissistic self-absorption.

The interconnection effect becomes most noticeable after about six weeks of consistent practice, when the individual areas begin to reinforce each other automatically. You'll find that your gratitude practice naturally includes appreciation for your relationships and your own growth. Your intuitive guidance will spontaneously consider how decisions affect the people you love. Your relationship interactions will automatically include wisdom you've learned and care for your own needs.

At this stage, personal development stops feeling like work you have to remember to do and starts feeling like a natural expression of who you are. The practices become self-reinforcing because each one makes the others more enjoyable and effective. This is when people typically report that the G.I.F.T.S. method feels different from other approaches they've tried. It becomes part of their identity rather than something they're trying to maintain through willpower.

The Implementation Infrastructure

The implementation infrastructure addresses the core problem that has derailed every previous attempt at sustainable change: the gap between initial enthusiasm and long-term follow-through. This system assumes that you will encounter resistance, forget practices, and face competing priorities that threaten your progress. Instead of treating these challenges as obstacles to overcome through better motivation or stronger discipline, the infrastructure treats them as predictable elements to work with through systematic responses.

The infrastructure operates through three interconnected components: tracking systems that provide objective feedback about your consistency, accountability structures that support you through difficult periods, and recovery protocols that get you back on track after inevitable lapses. Each component addresses a different aspect of the implementation process and together they create conditions where following through becomes easier than giving up.

The tracking component uses simple, objective measures that show you patterns in your behavior over time rather than requiring you to rely on subjective impressions of how you're doing. Most people dramatically underestimate how often they skip practices and overestimate how consistent they've been, leading to discouragement that feels justified but is based on inaccurate self-assessment.

Your tracking system will include a simple daily check-in that takes less than sixty seconds and focuses on completion rather than quality.

1. Did you do your gratitude practice today, regardless of how inspired or grateful you felt?
2. Did you pause to check in with your intuition before making at least one decision?
3. Did you have at least one meaningful interaction with someone you care about?
4. Did you capture or apply at least one insight?
5. Did you do at least one thing that demonstrated care for yourself?

These yes-or-no questions eliminate the subjective judgment that often leads to abandoning practices when they don't feel perfect or transformative. On days when your gratitude practice feels forced, you still get credit for doing it. When your intuitive guidance seems unclear, you still get credit for pausing to ask. This approach builds the consistency that creates long-term results rather than the perfection that creates short-term discouragement.

The tracking system also includes weekly and monthly reviews that help you identify patterns and adjust your approach based on what you learn about yourself. You might discover that you're most consistent with morning practices but struggle with evening ones, or that you maintain practices well during normal weeks but abandon them completely when traveling. This information allows you to modify your system to work with your actual patterns rather than fighting against them.

The accountability component recognizes that sustainable change rarely happens in isolation, but it doesn't depend on other people being available when you need support. Instead of relying on external accountability partners who might have their own inconsistencies, the system includes structured self-accountability that operates predictably regardless of other people's schedules or commitment levels.

Your accountability structure includes specific questions you ask yourself during weekly reviews, designed to maintain honest assessment without harsh self-criticism.

- What worked well this week in each of the five key areas?
- What challenges did you encounter and how did you respond?
- What do you want to adjust for next week based on what you learned?

These questions create the reflective awareness that allows you to course-correct quickly rather than drifting away from your practices gradually.

The system also includes celebration protocols that acknowledge progress in ways that motivate continued effort. Most people are quick to notice when they've missed practices but rarely acknowledge when they've been consistent. The accountability structure includes specific ways to recognize improvements, both small daily wins and larger monthly patterns of growth.

The recovery protocol represents the most innovative aspect of the implementation infrastructure because it treats lapses as normal parts of the change process rather than failures that invalidate your entire effort. Traditional approaches to habit formation suggest that missing practices creates setbacks that require starting over from the beginning. This all-or-nothing thinking leads many people to abandon their efforts entirely after relatively minor inconsistencies.

The G.I.F.T.S. recovery protocol includes specific actions to take on the day you notice you've been off track, regardless of how long the lapse has lasted.

The first step is acknowledging what happened without judgment or elaborate explanations. You simply notice that you stopped doing your practices and recognize this as information rather than evidence of personal failure.

The second step involves identifying the smallest possible action you can take immediately to reconnect with each of the five key areas. This might be appreciating something you can see from where you're sitting, asking your gut feeling about what to have for lunch, sending a brief message to someone you care about, writing down one thing you learned recently, or doing something kind for yourself. These micro-actions rebuild momentum without requiring the energy or time that might feel overwhelming when you're already behind.

The third step includes examining what led to the lapse without creating elaborate strategies to prevent it from happening again. Most lapses occur due to temporary circumstances like travel, illness, work deadlines, or family crises that don't require permanent changes to your system. The recovery protocol helps you distinguish between lapses that indicate you need to adjust your approach and lapses that simply reflect normal life fluctuations.

The implementation infrastructure also includes specific modifications for common life circumstances that typically derail personal development efforts. You'll have streamlined versions of all practices for busy periods, travel-friendly adaptations for when you're away from home, and simplified approaches for when you're dealing with stress or health challenges.

These modifications ensure that you can maintain some version of your practices regardless of circumstances, preventing the complete breaks that often lead to permanent abandonment. Even when you can only do abbreviated versions of your normal routine, you're maintaining the neural pathways and identity associations that make returning to full practices easier when circumstances improve.

The infrastructure evolves with you as the practices become more natural and require less conscious management. After several months of consistent implementation, you'll need less detailed tracking and can rely more on internal awareness of your patterns. The system includes guidance for gradually reducing external supports while maintaining the internal accountability that ensures continued growth.

Personal G.I.F.T.S. Assessment

Your personal assessment creates the foundation for everything that follows by establishing an honest baseline of where you currently stand in each of the five key areas. Most people have intuitive sense of their strengths and challenges, but this intuition is often distorted by self-criticism, social comparison, or wishful thinking. The assessment provides objective clarity that allows you to build on existing strengths while addressing genuine gaps.

The assessment process takes approximately thirty minutes and should be completed in one sitting to ensure consistency in your self-evaluation. Find a quiet space where you won't be interrupted and approach the questions with curiosity rather than judgment. The goal is accurate information that will guide your implementation strategy, not a report card that measures your worth as a person.

For the gratitude assessment, you'll evaluate both the frequency and authenticity of appreciation in your daily experience. Rate yourself on a scale of one to ten for each of these statements, where one means never true and ten means consistently true.

1. I notice and appreciate small positive moments throughout my day.
2. I feel genuinely grateful for my relationships, even when they're imperfect.
3. I can find something to appreciate even during difficult or stressful periods.
4. I express gratitude to others in ways that feel natural rather than forced.
5. I appreciate my own growth and progress rather than focusing primarily on what I haven't achieved yet.

Add your scores for a total between five and fifty. A score below twenty indicates that developing gratitude should be your primary initial focus. A score between twenty and thirty-five suggests moderate gratitude that could be deepened and made more consistent. A score above thirty-five indicates that gratitude is already a strength you can build on while focusing more attention on other areas.

The intuitive intention assessment evaluates how consistently you access and trust your inner guidance when making decisions. Rate yourself on these statements using the same one to ten scale.

1. I pause to check in with my gut feeling before making important decisions.
2. I can distinguish between fear-based reactions and wisdom-based responses.
3. I trust my intuition even when it conflicts with logical analysis.
4. I notice when my body is giving me information about people or situations.
5. I make decisions that feel right in my body, not just good on paper.

Your total score indicates your current relationship with intuitive guidance. Scores below twenty suggest that developing this capacity should be prioritized early in your implementation. Scores between twenty and thirty-five indicate moderate intuitive awareness that can be strengthened through consistent practice. Scores above thirty-five suggest that trusting your inner guidance is already well-developed and can support growth in other areas.

For family and friends connection, you'll assess both the depth and consistency of your relationships with the people who matter most to you. Rate these statements honestly, considering your overall patterns rather than recent exceptional moments.

1. I have regular, meaningful conversations with the people I care about most.
2. I feel comfortable being vulnerable and authentic in my close relationships.
3. I make time for relationships even when work and other obligations are demanding.
4. I express appreciation and affection to family and friends regularly.
5. I feel genuinely supported and understood by the important people in

my life.

Relationship scores below twenty indicate that this area needs significant attention and may be contributing to feelings of isolation or disconnection in other areas of your life. Scores between twenty and thirty-five suggest good relationships that could be deepened through more intentional attention. Scores above thirty-five indicate strong relationship foundations that can support your growth in other areas.

The treasured wisdom assessment evaluates how effectively you capture insights from your experiences and apply them to improve your daily life. Consider how consistently these statements describe your current patterns.

1. I regularly capture insights from books, conversations, and experiences rather than just consuming them passively.
2. I have systems for reviewing and reflecting on what I've learned.
3. I can identify specific ways that wisdom I've gained has changed how I handle situations.
4. I actively look for opportunities to apply insights rather than just collecting them intellectually.
5. I learn from my mistakes and challenges rather than just enduring them.

Scores below twenty suggest that you may be consuming wisdom without integrating it, leading to the knowing-doing gap that motivated you to read this book. Scores between twenty and thirty-five indicate moderate applied wisdom that can be systematized for greater effectiveness. Scores above thirty-five suggest strong learning integration that can accelerate your progress in other areas.

For self-love and care, you'll assess how consistently you treat yourself with kindness and meet your own needs. This area is often the most challenging for people to evaluate accurately because self-criticism can distort perception in either direction. Rate these statements based on your actual behavior patterns rather than your intentions or values.

1. I speak to myself with the same kindness I would show a good friend.
2. I prioritize meeting my basic needs for rest, nutrition, and movement.
3. I set boundaries that protect my time and energy from excessive demands.
4. I celebrate my progress and accomplishments rather than only focusing on what needs improvement.
5. I make choices that honor my authentic needs and values rather than just meeting external expectations.

Self-care scores below twenty indicate that this foundational area needs immediate attention, as self-neglect undermines progress in all other areas. Scores between twenty and thirty-five suggest inconsistent self-care that becomes more difficult during stressful periods. Scores above thirty-five indicate solid self-care foundations that support sustainable growth in other areas.

After completing all five assessments, you'll identify your strongest area to use as an anchor for building the others, and your weakest area to prioritize for initial improvement. Your strongest area becomes the foundation you can rely on during challenging periods and the source of motivation when other practices feel difficult. Your weakest area receives focused attention first because improvements there will have disproportionate positive effects on your overall experience.

The assessment also reveals common patterns that affect implementation strategy. If all your scores are relatively similar, you can work on all five key areas simultaneously from the beginning. If there are significant gaps between areas, you'll start with your weakest area while maintaining your strongest one, then gradually add the others as your capacity increases.

Record your scores and initial observations in writing, as you'll return to this assessment every three months to track your progress and adjust your focus as needed. Most people are surprised by how much their scores improve after consistent implementation, and reviewing your initial assessment provides concrete evidence of growth that maintains motivation during challenging periods.

Your Implementation Process

The G.I.F.T.S. method succeeds where other personal development approaches fail because it treats transformation as an integrated system rather than a collection of separate practices. The five key areas: gratitude, intuitive intention, family and friends connection, treasured wisdom, and self-love and care, naturally reinforce each other when developed simultaneously, creating sustainable change that feels organic rather than forced.

Your assessment has revealed your current strengths and gaps across all five key areas, providing the foundation for a personalized implementation strategy. The implementation infrastructure ensures that you'll actually follow through on your intentions through systematic tracking, accountability, and recovery protocols that treat resistance and lapses as normal parts of the change process rather than failures that invalidate your efforts.

Your first implementation step is to set up your tracking system using a simple format that takes less than sixty seconds per day. Create a document or use a notebook where you can record daily yes-or-no answers to five questions.

1. Did I practice gratitude today?
2. Did I check in with my intuition before at least one decision?
3. Did I have a connection with someone I care about?
4. Did I capture or apply wisdom?
5. Did I do something that demonstrated self-care?

These questions focus on completion rather than quality, eliminating the subjective judgment that often leads to abandoning practices when they don't feel perfect. On days when your practices feel forced or uninspired, you still get credit for doing them. This builds the consistency that creates long-term transformation rather than the perfection that creates short-term discouragement.

Your second step is to identify your anchor area and your priority area based on your assessment scores. Your anchor area is your highest-scoring category, which you'll maintain and build on throughout your implementation. Your priority area is your lowest-scoring category, which will receive focused attention during your first month of practice.

If your scores are relatively similar across all areas, choose gratitude as your anchor because it creates the foundation that makes all other practices more accessible. If you have significant gaps between areas, focus your initial energy on bringing your weakest area up to a moderate level before expanding your attention to other categories.

Your third step is to design your recovery protocol for when you inevitably miss practices or drift away from your routine. Write down the smallest possible action you can take in each area to reconnect after a lapse. These micro-actions should require less than one minute each and be doable regardless of your circumstances or energy level.

For gratitude, this might be appreciating something you can see from wherever you are. For intuitive intention, this might be asking your gut feeling about what to do next. For relationships, this might be sending a brief message to someone you care about. For wisdom, this might be writing down one thing you learned recently. For self-care, this might be taking three deep breaths or drinking a glass of water.

Your fourth step is to schedule your first weekly review, which will take place seven days from today at a specific time you choose now. During this review, you'll look at your daily tracking responses and ask yourself what worked well, what challenges you encountered, and what you want to adjust for the following week. This review creates the reflective awareness that allows you to course-correct quickly rather than drifting away from your practices gradually.

Your final step is to begin tomorrow with a simple integrated practice that addresses all five key areas in less than five minutes.

1. Start your day by appreciating three things you can see, hear, or feel

from wherever you wake up.

2. Ask your intuition what it wants you to know about the day ahead.
3. Think of one person you care about and send them appreciation, either mentally or through a brief message.
4. Recall one piece of wisdom that could be useful today.
5. Do one small thing that demonstrates care for yourself, such as stretching, drinking water, or speaking to yourself kindly about the day ahead.

This integrated morning practice establishes the foundation from which everything else emerges and demonstrates the interconnection effect that makes the G.I.F.T.S. method so powerful. Each element supports and strengthens the others, creating momentum that makes sustainable transformation feel inevitable rather than effortful.

4

G is for GRATITUDE

You've tried gratitude practices before. Maybe you wrote three things you were thankful for each morning, or kept a gratitude journal, or attempted to appreciate your life more consciously. For a while, it might have felt good, even transformative. Then gradually, the practice started feeling forced, mechanical, almost insulting to your intelligence. You found yourself struggling to think of things to write down, repeating the same items day after day, or abandoning the practice entirely when life got stressful.

This experience doesn't mean gratitude doesn't work or that you're ungrateful by nature. It means you were practicing gratitude as a mental exercise rather than a way of being, trying to think your way into appreciation rather than living from a place where gratitude emerges naturally. The difference between these two approaches determines whether gratitude becomes a sustainable foundation for transformation or another abandoned self-improvement technique.

Real gratitude isn't something you do for five minutes each morning before returning to your normal perspective for the rest of the day. It's a fundamental shift in how you interpret your experience that affects every interaction, decision, and response throughout your life. When gratitude becomes integrated into your identity, you don't have to remember to be thankful. You naturally notice what's working, what's beautiful, and what's meaningful because that's how grateful people see the world.

This chapter will show you how to make that shift from performative gratitude exercises to authentic appreciation that transforms your daily experience. You'll learn why your previous attempts felt forced and fake, discover a simple integration method that weaves gratitude into moments you're already living, and understand how genuine appreciation becomes your relationship superpower and the foundation that supports all other areas of the G.I.F.T.S. method.

Why Your Gratitude Practice Isn't Working

Most gratitude practices fail because they treat appreciation like a cognitive exercise rather than an emotional and physiological state. You sit down with your journal, think about what you should be grateful for, and write down items that make logical sense: your health, your family, your job, your home. These are genuinely good things in your life, but approaching them through mental analysis rather than felt experience creates a disconnect between what you write and what you actually feel.

Your nervous system can distinguish between authentic appreciation and intellectual acknowledgment of good fortune. When you force yourself to feel grateful for things you think you should appreciate, your body recognizes the incongruence and resists the practice as inauthentic. This resistance shows up as boredom with the exercise, difficulty thinking of new things to write, or the sense that you're going through meaningless motions.

The problem deepens when you use gratitude practices to try to fix negative emotions or difficult circumstances rather than to genuinely appreciate what's actually working in your life. If you're struggling with loneliness, financial stress, or relationship conflicts, writing down that you're grateful for your health and home can feel like you're trying to convince yourself that your problems don't matter or that you shouldn't feel upset about real challenges.

This approach turns gratitude into a form of spiritual bypassing, where you attempt to think positive thoughts instead of dealing with actual issues that need attention. Your deeper wisdom recognizes this avoidance strategy and creates internal resistance that makes the practice feel forced and ineffective. You end up feeling worse about yourself for being unable to maintain appreciation for obvious blessings, adding self-criticism to whatever challenges you were already facing.

Another common problem occurs when gratitude practices become performance rather than genuine appreciation. You might find yourself thinking about what would sound good to write down, what would make you seem appropriately grateful, or what would fit with the image of someone who has their life together. This performance orientation disconnects you from your actual experience and turns gratitude into another way to judge yourself rather than a practice that opens your heart.

The timing of most gratitude practices also works against their effectiveness. When you sit down specifically to practice gratitude, you're often in a different emotional state than the one you want to cultivate throughout your day. You might feel calm and reflective during your morning practice, but stressed and reactive during your afternoon meetings. The appreciation you generated during your designated gratitude time doesn't transfer to moments when you actually need it most.

Many people also make gratitude practices too elaborate and time-consuming to maintain consistently. You might start with ambitious plans to write detailed reflections about why you appreciate each item, or to include photos, or to share your gratitude with others daily. These elaborate systems require more energy and time than the actual appreciation they're designed to cultivate, making them unsustainable when life gets busy or stressful.

The focus on quantity rather than quality in many gratitude approaches also undermines their effectiveness. When you're trying to think of three or five or ten things to be grateful for, you often end up listing items that don't actually generate genuine appreciation. It's better to feel authentic gratitude for one thing than to intellectually acknowledge ten things that don't move you emotionally.

Perhaps most importantly, traditional gratitude practices often operate in isolation from the rest of your life rather than being integrated with your relationships, decision-making, and daily activities. When gratitude exists as a separate practice that you do alone for a few minutes, it doesn't have the opportunity to transform how you interact with people, handle challenges, or make choices throughout your day.

Real gratitude emerges from paying attention to your actual experience with openness and curiosity rather than from trying to generate appreciation for things you think you should value. It develops through noticing small moments of beauty, connection, or satisfaction that are already happening in your life but usually pass by unacknowledged because you're focused on problems, goals, or distractions.

The shift from forced gratitude to natural appreciation happens when you learn to recognize and savor positive experiences as they occur rather than trying to manufacture them during designated practice times. This requires developing the capacity to notice when something feels good, meaningful, or beautiful, and allowing yourself to fully experience that positive feeling instead of immediately moving on to the next task or worry.

This approach works because it builds on emotions and experiences that are already present rather than trying to create feelings that aren't there. When you notice that your morning coffee tastes particularly good, that your conversation with a colleague was genuinely enjoyable, or that the light coming through your window is beautiful, you're working with authentic appreciation rather than manufactured thankfulness.

The Gratitude Integration Method

The integration method transforms gratitude from a separate practice into a natural response by weaving appreciation into moments and activities that are already part of your daily routine. Instead of setting aside specific time to think grateful thoughts, you learn to notice and savor positive experiences as they happen throughout your day. This creates a foundation of appreciation that builds gradually and sustainably rather than depending on your ability to maintain a separate practice.

The method begins with identifying three transition moments that already exist in your daily schedule. Times when you're naturally shifting from one activity to another and your mind is relatively open to new input. Common transition moments include the first sip of your morning coffee, getting into your car, washing your hands, or the moment you sit down at your desk. These transitions happen automatically every day, making them perfect anchors for developing gratitude habits.

During each transition moment, you pause for just ten to fifteen seconds to notice something you can genuinely appreciate about your immediate experience. This might be the warmth of your coffee cup in your hands, the comfort of your car seat, the feeling of clean hands, or the fact that you have work that provides for your needs. The key is focusing on sensory experiences or immediate circumstances rather than abstract concepts or distant blessings.

This sensory focus works because your body can generate authentic appreciation for things you're actually experiencing in the moment. When you notice that your coffee smells rich and inviting, your nervous system responds with genuine pleasure that doesn't require mental effort to maintain. When you appreciate the comfort of sitting down after standing, you're acknowledging a real physical experience that naturally generates positive feelings.

The brevity of these appreciation moments is crucial for sustainability. Fifteen seconds is long enough to generate authentic gratitude but short enough that you can maintain the practice even during busy or stressful periods. You're not trying to have profound spiritual experiences or life-changing insights. You're simply noticing and acknowledging positive aspects of your ordinary experience.

As these micro-appreciations become automatic during your chosen transition moments, they begin to shift your overall perceptual habits. Your nervous system learns to scan for positive aspects of your experience rather than only noticing problems, threats, or inadequacies. This happens gradually and unconsciously, without requiring conscious effort to maintain a positive attitude or forcing yourself to see the bright side of difficult situations.

The second component of the integration method involves appreciation during routine activities rather than adding new practices to your schedule. While brushing your teeth, you might appreciate having clean water and dental care that keeps you healthy. While preparing meals, you might notice the colors and textures of your food or feel grateful for having nourishment available. While walking from one place to another, you might appreciate your body's ability to move or notice something beautiful in your environment.

This approach leverages activities you're already doing every day rather than requiring additional time or energy for gratitude practice. Since you're going to brush your teeth anyway, appreciating the experience doesn't add to your schedule or create another item on your to-do list. The gratitude emerges from paying attention to activities you're already engaged in rather than from separate practices you have to remember to do.

The method also includes appreciation for challenges and difficulties, but only after you've established a foundation of gratitude for obviously positive experiences. When you're consistently noticing and appreciating good moments throughout your day, you develop the emotional capacity to find meaning and growth opportunities in difficult situations without bypassing legitimate concerns or feelings.

This advanced appreciation might involve recognizing how a work challenge is helping you develop new skills, appreciating the intimacy that comes from supporting a friend through difficulty, or finding gratitude for your body's wisdom in getting sick when you need to rest. These appreciations emerge naturally from a grateful perspective rather than from trying to force positive interpretations of negative experiences.

The integration method includes specific approaches for maintaining gratitude during stressful periods when appreciation feels difficult or inappropriate. Instead of abandoning gratitude entirely during challenging times, you shift to appreciating smaller, more immediate experiences like the taste of water when you're thirsty, the relief of sitting down when you're tired, or the comfort of breathing deeply when you're anxious.

These stress-period appreciations serve as anchors that keep you connected to positive aspects of your experience even when larger circumstances are difficult. They don't minimize or dismiss your challenges, but they prevent stress from completely overwhelming your capacity to notice what's still working in your life. This balanced approach maintains your gratitude foundation without creating pressure to feel positive about everything.

This method also incorporates appreciation for your own growth and efforts rather than only focusing on external circumstances. You might appreciate your courage in having a difficult conversation, your persistence in maintaining healthy habits, or your compassion in supporting someone else. Self-appreciation builds a positive relationship with yourself that supports all other areas of the G.I.F.T.S. method.

Weekly integration reviews help you notice patterns in what generates authentic appreciation versus what feels forced or artificial. You might discover that you feel genuine gratitude for sensory experiences but struggle to appreciate abstract concepts, or that you naturally appreciate relationships but have difficulty with material circumstances. This self-knowledge allows you to focus your gratitude practice on areas where appreciation flows naturally while gradually expanding into more challenging territories.

The ultimate goal of the integration method is for gratitude to become so natural that you no longer think of it as a practice you're maintaining. Appreciation becomes your default response to positive experiences, and you automatically notice beauty, kindness, and meaning throughout your day. This shift typically takes three to six months of consistent integration, after which grateful living feels effortless rather than effortful.

Gratitude as Your Relationship Superpower

Gratitude transforms your relationships more powerfully than any communication technique or conflict resolution strategy because it shifts the fundamental energy you bring to every interaction. When you approach people from a place of genuine appreciation rather than need, criticism, or expectation, you create emotional safety that allows others to show up more authentically and generously in response to your presence.

Most people interact with family and friends from a subtle foundation of noticing what's missing, what could be better, or what they wish was different. You might appreciate your partner intellectually while focusing emotionally on ways they could be more attentive, supportive, or understanding. You might love your children deeply while spending most interactions correcting, instructing, or worrying about their choices and development.

This gap between intellectual appreciation and emotional focus creates relationships that feel effortful and unsatisfying for everyone involved. People sense when they're being evaluated or improved rather than genuinely appreciated, and they respond by becoming defensive, distant, or resentful. Even when your intentions are loving, approaching relationships from a foundation of what's lacking rather than what's wonderful creates disconnection and conflict.

Gratitude-based relating involves learning to see and acknowledge what's already beautiful, funny, kind, or admirable about the people in your life rather than primarily focusing on what you want them to change. This doesn't mean ignoring legitimate concerns or avoiding necessary conversations about problems, but it means establishing appreciation as the foundation from which everything else emerges.

The practice begins with specific appreciation rather than generic compliments or acknowledgments. Instead of telling your partner "I appreciate you," you might say "I appreciate how you always make sure we have good coffee in the morning" or "I love watching you get excited about your projects." Instead of telling your teenager "You're a good kid," you might notice "I appreciate how you helped your sister with her homework without being asked."

This specificity works because it shows that you're actually paying attention to who they are and what they do rather than offering automatic praise or trying to make them feel better. People can distinguish between genuine appreciation that reflects real observation and generic positivity that could apply to anyone. Specific gratitude creates the feeling of being truly seen and valued for their unique qualities and contributions.

The timing of relationship gratitude matters as much as the content. Expressing appreciation immediately when you notice something wonderful is much more powerful than saving it for special occasions or designated appreciation conversations. When your friend makes you laugh during an ordinary phone call, acknowledging your enjoyment in that moment creates connection that wouldn't happen if you mentioned it weeks later.

This immediate appreciation also helps you notice positive qualities and behaviors that you might otherwise take for granted or forget by the time you have an opportunity to mention them. Most people are much better at remembering what annoyed or disappointed them than what delighted or impressed them, so real-time gratitude helps balance your perception toward a more accurate and positive view of your relationships.

Gratitude also transforms how you handle relationship challenges and conflicts by maintaining appreciation for the person even when you're addressing problems with their behavior. When you need to have a difficult conversation with someone you love, starting from a foundation of genuine appreciation for who they are creates emotional safety that makes them more receptive to hearing your concerns.

This might involve beginning challenging conversations with authentic acknowledgment of what you value about your relationship before addressing what needs to change. "I love how we can usually talk through anything together, and I'm hoping we can figure out this situation with the same openness," creates a completely different dynamic than launching directly into complaints or demands.

The approach also includes appreciating people's positive intentions even when their actions create problems or hurt feelings. Your teenage daughter might choose friends you're concerned about, but you can appreciate her loyalty and desire for connection even while discussing your worries. Your partner might handle money in ways that stress you, but you can acknowledge their generosity and desire to provide, even while working out budgeting disagreements.

This appreciation for positive intentions doesn't excuse harmful behavior or eliminate the need for boundaries and changes, but it creates a foundation of respect that makes problem-solving more effective. People are more willing to examine their behavior and consider changes when they feel appreciated for who they are rather than judged for what they're doing wrong.

Gratitude-based relating also involves appreciating the growth and changes you see in people rather than holding them to past versions of themselves or focusing on areas where they haven't progressed. Your spouse might still struggle with organization, but you can notice and acknowledge the efforts they're making rather than only seeing what remains unchanged. Your friend might still make impulsive decisions, but you can appreciate their increasing willingness to ask for advice.

This growth-focused appreciation encourages continued positive development because people tend to live up to the version of themselves that others see and acknowledge. When you notice and express gratitude for someone's progress, patience, or effort, you reinforce those qualities and make them more likely to continue developing in positive directions.

The relationship benefits of gratitude extend beyond your immediate family and close friends to casual interactions with colleagues, neighbors, and strangers. When you approach people with appreciation for their helpfulness, competence, or kindness, you create positive experiences that brighten everyone's day and make ordinary interactions more pleasant and meaningful.

This expanded gratitude practice might involve thanking the cashier who handles your transaction efficiently, appreciating the colleague who answers your questions patiently, or acknowledging the neighbor who keeps their yard beautiful. These small appreciations create ripple effects of positivity that improve the social environment for everyone while strengthening your own capacity for noticing and expressing gratitude.

Over time, gratitude-based relating changes how people respond to you because they associate your presence with feeling appreciated and valued. Family members look forward to spending time with you because they know they'll feel seen and acknowledged rather than criticized. Friends seek out your company because they feel better about themselves when they're with you. Colleagues enjoy working with you because you notice and appreciate their contributions.

This positive cycle creates relationships that feel nourishing and energizing rather than draining and effortful. Instead of constantly working to fix problems or manage conflicts, you spend most of your relational energy enjoying and appreciating the good qualities that are already present in the people you love.

The Gratitude Momentum Effect

Consistent gratitude practice creates momentum that extends far beyond appreciation itself, naturally enhancing your intuitive capacity and self-compassion in ways that make all other areas of personal development more accessible and effective. This momentum effect explains why gratitude often becomes the foundation that supports transformation in every other area of life, even when you're not consciously trying to improve those areas.

The physiological changes that occur with regular gratitude practice create optimal conditions for accessing intuitive guidance. When you consistently appreciate your experience rather than constantly scanning for problems or threats, your nervous system shifts out of chronic stress response and into a state of open awareness. Your heart rate variability improves, your cortisol levels decrease, and your prefrontal cortex becomes more active while your amygdala calms down.

These biological shifts quiet the mental noise and emotional reactivity that typically obscure subtle inner signals. Your gut feelings become more noticeable when you're not overwhelmed by anxiety or criticism. Your sense of what feels right or wrong becomes clearer when you're approaching decisions from appreciation rather than scarcity or fear. Your ability to distinguish between wisdom-based responses and reaction-based impulses improves dramatically when your overall emotional state is positive and stable.

The momentum effect also enhances your capacity to recognize and apply wisdom from your experiences because gratitude naturally creates the reflective awareness that allows learning to occur. When you appreciate challenges as opportunities for growth rather than just problems to endure, you automatically look for lessons and insights that can improve how you handle similar situations in the future.

This learning orientation emerges organically from a grateful perspective rather than from forcing yourself to find positive meanings in negative experiences. When you genuinely appreciate your resilience in getting through a difficult period, you naturally notice what strategies and resources helped you cope effectively. When you feel grateful for the support you received during a crisis, you automatically recognize the value of asking for help and maintaining strong relationships.

Gratitude also builds the self-respect and confidence that makes applying wisdom feel natural rather than risky. When you regularly appreciate your own efforts, growth, and positive qualities, you develop trust in your ability to handle challenges and make good decisions. This self-trust creates the emotional foundation that allows you to act on insights even when they require stepping outside your comfort zone or changing familiar patterns.

The momentum extends to self-compassion because grateful people naturally treat themselves with the same kindness they feel toward others they appreciate. When you consistently notice what's working in your life and acknowledge your own contributions to positive outcomes, self-criticism becomes less automatic, and self-care becomes more obvious. You start speaking to yourself the way you would speak to someone you genuinely appreciate rather than someone you're constantly trying to improve.

This self-compassion creates an upward spiral where treating yourself kindly makes it easier to maintain gratitude practices, which strengthens your capacity for self-appreciation, which supports more consistent self-care. Instead of using gratitude to compensate for self-neglect or to convince yourself that your needs don't matter, appreciation becomes the foundation for valuing and caring for yourself appropriately.

The momentum effect becomes particularly noticeable during challenging periods when people who have established gratitude foundations maintain emotional stability and problem-solving capacity much better than those who haven't developed appreciation practices. Instead of being overwhelmed by difficulties, grateful people automatically look for resources, support, and opportunities that can help them navigate challenges more effectively.

This resilience doesn't come from denying problems or forcing positive attitudes, but from having developed the capacity to notice what's still working even when significant things are going wrong. Someone dealing with job loss might appreciate their health, their relationships, and their skills even while acknowledging the stress and uncertainty of their situation. This balanced perspective maintains hope and energy for taking constructive action rather than becoming paralyzed by focusing only on what's not working.

The momentum also creates what researchers call "broaden and build" effects, where positive emotions like gratitude expand your awareness and build psychological resources that support long-term flourishing. When you feel genuinely appreciative, you notice more opportunities, connect more easily with other people, think more creatively about solutions to problems, and maintain energy for pursuing meaningful goals.

These expanded capacities accumulate over time, creating compound benefits that extend far beyond the immediate pleasure of feeling grateful. People who maintain gratitude practices for several months typically report improvements in their relationships, decision-making, stress management, and overall life satisfaction that they didn't expect when they started focusing on appreciation.

The momentum effect also influences how other people respond to you, creating external conditions that support continued growth and positive change. When you consistently approach life from appreciation rather than complaint or criticism, you attract people and opportunities that align with that positive energy. Colleagues want to work with you on interesting projects, friends invite you to enjoyable activities, and family members feel more comfortable sharing good news and asking for support.

This positive social feedback reinforces your gratitude practice and creates environmental conditions that make maintaining appreciation easier and more natural. Instead of swimming against a current of negativity and criticism, you find yourself in social and professional environments that support and encourage the positive perspective you're cultivating.

The ultimate momentum effect is that gratitude becomes self-reinforcing rather than requiring ongoing conscious effort to maintain. When appreciation consistently leads to better relationships, clearer guidance, more effective learning, and greater self-compassion, continuing the practice feels obvious and rewarding rather than disciplined and effortful. You maintain gratitude not because you should or because it's good for you, but because grateful living creates the kind of life you actually want to experience.

Gratitude Implementation Process

Gratitude becomes transformative when you shift from thinking thankful thoughts during designated practice times to living from a foundation of genuine appreciation that emerges naturally throughout your day. The integration method weaves gratitude into transition moments and routine activities you're already experiencing, creating sustainable appreciation that doesn't require additional time or energy to maintain. When gratitude becomes authentic rather than performative, it serves as your relationship superpower and creates momentum that naturally enhances your intuitive capacity and self-compassion.

Your first implementation step is to identify three transition moments in your daily routine where you can pause for ten to fifteen seconds to appreciate something about your immediate experience. Choose transitions that happen automatically every day, such as your first sip of coffee, getting into your car, washing your hands, or sitting down at your desk. These moments become anchors for developing appreciation habits that integrate seamlessly into your existing schedule.

During each transition moment, focus on sensory experiences or immediate circumstances rather than abstract concepts or distant blessings. Appreciate the warmth of your coffee cup, the comfort of your car seat, the feeling of clean hands, or the fact that you have meaningful work. This sensory focus generates authentic gratitude that your nervous system recognizes as genuine rather than manufactured.

Your second step is to practice specific appreciation with one person you care about every day for the next week. Instead of generic compliments or acknowledgments, notice and express gratitude for particular qualities, actions, or contributions that you genuinely value. Tell your partner you appreciate how they always remember to ask about your day, or thank your colleague for explaining something patiently, or acknowledge your friend for being someone you can count on for honest advice.

Express this appreciation immediately when you notice it, rather than saving it for special occasions or designated gratitude conversations. Real-time acknowledgment creates a connection and shows that you're paying attention to who they are and what they do rather than offering automatic praise or trying to make them feel better.

Your third step is to establish appreciation during one routine activity that you already do daily. While brushing your teeth, preparing meals, or walking from one place to another, notice something you can genuinely appreciate about the experience. This might be having access to clean water and dental care, enjoying the colors and textures of your food, or appreciating your body's ability to move you where you need to go.

The key is leveraging activities you're already engaged in rather than adding separate gratitude practices to your schedule. Since you're going to brush your teeth anyway, appreciating the experience doesn't create another item on your to-do list but simply involves paying attention to an activity you're already doing.

Your fourth step is to practice stress-period gratitude by appreciating smaller, more immediate experiences when larger circumstances feel challenging. Instead of trying to feel grateful for difficult situations themselves, notice positive aspects of your immediate experience like the taste of water when you're thirsty, the relief of sitting down when you're tired, or the comfort of breathing deeply when you're anxious.

These micro-appreciations serve as anchors that maintain your connection to positive aspects of experience even during challenging times. They don't minimize your difficulties but prevent stress from completely overwhelming your capacity to notice what's still working in your life.

Your final step is to begin your weekly gratitude review by reflecting on patterns in what generates authentic appreciation versus what feels forced or artificial. Notice whether you feel genuine gratitude for sensory experiences, relationships, personal growth, or material circumstances, and use this self-knowledge to focus your practice on areas where appreciation flows naturally while gradually expanding into more challenging territories.

Track your gratitude integration using the simple daily question from your G.I.F.T.S. tracking system: **"Did I practice gratitude today?"** This yes-or-no response focuses on completion rather than quality, giving you credit for noticing and appreciating anything, regardless of how profound or transformative the experience felt. Consistent appreciation, even when it feels ordinary or small, builds the foundation for the momentum effects that support transformation in all other areas of your life.

5

I is for INTUITIVE INTENTION

You make hundreds of decisions every day, from what to wear and what to eat to how to respond to emails and which projects deserve your attention. Most of these choices get filtered through endless mental analysis, weighing pros and cons, seeking advice from others, and second-guessing yourself even after you've decided. This overthinking approach leaves you feeling exhausted, uncertain, and disconnected from the deeper wisdom that could guide you toward choices that actually feel right in your body.

Somewhere along the way, you learned that good decisions come from logical analysis and careful consideration of all available information. You were taught to distrust gut feelings as unreliable, emotional, or naive compared to rational thought processes. This conditioning served you well in academic and professional settings where analytical thinking is valued, but it also disconnected you from an intelligence system that often knows things your conscious mind hasn't figured out yet.

Your intuitive guidance system operates faster than conscious thought, drawing on pattern recognition, emotional intelligence, and subtle environmental cues that your analytical mind processes too slowly to be useful in real-time decision-making. When you override this inner guidance consistently, you end up making choices that look good on paper but feel wrong in your life, leading to the disconnect between external success and internal satisfaction that characterizes so many accomplished people.

This chapter will show you how to rebuild trust in your inner guidance system while maintaining your analytical abilities as valuable tools rather than the only source of wisdom available to you. You'll learn to distinguish between fear-based mental noise and genuine intuitive signals, develop practices for accessing your inner wisdom throughout the day, and discover how trusting your gut feelings actually leads to better outcomes than overthinking alone.

Why You're Not Listening

Your disconnection from your inner guidance didn't happen overnight but developed gradually through years of being rewarded for analytical thinking while having your gut feelings dismissed, corrected, or ignored by authority figures who meant well but didn't understand the value of inner guidance. Every time a teacher told you to show your work instead of trusting that you knew the right answer, every time a parent questioned your instincts about people or situations, every time a boss asked for data to support decisions you knew were right, you learned to doubt your inner knowing.

The educational system that shaped your thinking patterns was designed to develop logical reasoning and evidence-based decision-making, which are genuinely valuable skills for many life situations. But this same system often treated intuitive insights as inferior to analytical conclusions, creating the impression that gut feelings are unreliable guides compared to careful rational analysis. You learned to value thoughts over feelings, logic over instinct, and external validation over internal knowing.

This conditioning was reinforced by a culture that celebrates people who can defend their choices with data and reasoning while viewing those who follow their intuition as impulsive, emotional, or naive. You absorbed the message that successful people make decisions based on facts and analysis rather than feelings and hunches, even though research shows that the most effective leaders and entrepreneurs consistently rely on intuitive guidance to navigate complex situations where complete information isn't available.

The pace of modern life also works against developing intuitive awareness because inner guidance emerges most clearly when your nervous system is calm and your attention is focused inward. The constant stimulation from phones, emails, social media, and packed schedules keeps your mind busy with external input and reactive thinking, leaving little space for the quiet awareness where subtle inner signals become noticeable.

When you're always rushing from one obligation to another, checking messages, and managing multiple priorities simultaneously, you don't have the mental space to pause and sense what feels right about the choices you're making. Your decisions get made quickly based on immediate pressures and logical considerations rather than deeper wisdom about what would serve your authentic needs and long-term wellbeing.

People-pleasing patterns also disconnect you from inner guidance because they train you to prioritize other people's expectations and reactions over your own sense of what feels right. When you consistently override your gut feelings to avoid disappointing others or to maintain approval, you gradually lose touch with your authentic preferences and desires. Your inner guidance system becomes clouded by anxiety about external reactions rather than clear about your internal truth.

This people-pleasing dynamic is particularly destructive because it teaches you to distrust the very signals that would help you create healthy boundaries and authentic relationships. Your intuition might tell you that someone is being manipulative or that a request feels inappropriate, but you override these signals to be nice or accommodating, then wonder why you feel resentful or taken advantage of later.

Past experiences where following your intuition led to negative outcomes also create resistance to trusting inner guidance in the future. Maybe you had a gut feeling about a relationship that turned out badly anyway, or you followed your instincts about a career choice that didn't work out as expected. These experiences can create the conclusion that your intuition is unreliable, even though the negative outcomes might have occurred because you didn't follow your guidance completely or because external circumstances changed in unpredictable ways.

The problem with this reasoning is that it ignores all the times your intuition was accurate and helpful while focusing only on apparent failures. You probably don't remember the countless occasions when your gut feelings steered you away from problems, helped you connect with the right people, or guided you toward opportunities that served you well. Negative experiences get more attention and memory space than positive ones, creating a distorted impression of your intuitive accuracy.

Perfectionism also undermines trust in inner guidance because it demands certainty and guaranteed outcomes that intuition cannot provide. Your analytical mind wants to know exactly what will happen if you follow a particular course of action, but intuitive guidance often points you toward choices that feel right without providing detailed predictions about results. When you need absolute certainty before taking action, you'll always choose analysis over intuition because logic promises more control over outcomes.

This demand for certainty ignores the reality that most important life decisions involve unknown variables and unpredictable factors that no amount of analysis can fully account for. Your intuition specializes in navigating uncertainty by sensing what feels aligned with your authentic self and deeper values, even when you can't predict or control external outcomes. Trusting this guidance requires accepting that you can make good choices without knowing exactly where they'll lead.

The fear of being judged for making intuition-based decisions also keeps many people stuck in overthinking patterns. When you follow your gut feelings and things don't work out perfectly, you worry that others will see you as impulsive or irresponsible. When you make analytical decisions that fail, you can at least defend your reasoning process, even if the outcome was disappointing. This social protection makes overthinking feel safer than trusting inner wisdom, even when overthinking consistently leads to choices that feel wrong.

Rebuilding trust in your intuitive guidance requires recognizing that the disconnection happened for understandable reasons and doesn't reflect a fundamental flaw in your inner wisdom system. Your intuition is still operating and providing valuable information. You've simply learned to ignore or override it in favor of mental analysis. The capacity for inner knowing hasn't disappeared; it just needs to be acknowledged, developed, and integrated with your analytical abilities rather than replaced by them.

Reconnecting With Your Intuitive Voice

Your intuitive voice communicates through physical sensations, emotional responses, and sudden knowing that emerges before your rational mind has time to analyze situations completely. Learning to recognize and trust these signals requires developing body awareness and emotional intelligence that most people never learned because they were taught to prioritize thinking over feeling as a source of reliable information about their choices and circumstances.

The reconnection process begins with understanding that your body is constantly receiving and processing information about your environment, relationships, and decisions through subtle cues that your conscious mind doesn't register directly. Your nervous system picks up on facial expressions, vocal tones, energy levels, and environmental factors that influence how safe, comfortable, or excited you feel in different situations, even when you can't articulate why you're having those responses.

Physical sensations provide some of the clearest and most immediate intuitive guidance available to you. Your stomach might tighten when someone is being dishonest, even if their words sound convincing. Your chest might feel open and expansive when you're considering a choice that aligns with your authentic desires. Your shoulders might tense when you're about to agree to something that violates your boundaries, even if you can't explain logically why the request feels inappropriate.

Learning to notice these body signals requires slowing down enough to pay attention to your physical experience rather than staying focused entirely on mental activity. This means pausing periodically throughout your day to check in with how your body feels, especially when you're making decisions or interacting with people. The pause only needs to last a few seconds, just long enough to notice whether you feel relaxed or tense, open or contracted, energized or drained.

Emotional responses also carry intuitive information that gets overlooked when you focus primarily on logical analysis. Sudden enthusiasm about an opportunity might indicate that it aligns with your authentic interests and values, even if you can't explain rationally why it appeals to you. Unexpected anxiety about a choice that looks good on paper might signal that something important is missing from your analysis or that the timing isn't right for that particular direction.

The key to working with emotional guidance is distinguishing between reactions based on past conditioning and responses that reflect present-moment wisdom. Fear about taking risks often comes from old programming about safety and approval rather than accurate assessment of current circumstances. But unease about specific people or situations frequently contains valuable information about dynamics that your conscious mind hasn't recognized yet.

Sudden knowing represents the most direct form of intuitive guidance, appearing as clear understanding or certainty about what to do without going through a logical reasoning process. You might suddenly know that you need to call a friend who's been on your mind, or that a job opportunity isn't right for you despite attractive benefits, or that a relationship needs more attention even though everything seems fine on the surface.

This immediate knowing often feels different from mental conclusions because it arrives complete and doesn't require building up through analysis or evidence gathering. The challenge is learning to trust these insights even when you can't explain or defend them to others who might ask for your reasoning. The guidance is often accurate, but it requires acting on incomplete information and accepting that you might not understand why something is right until after you follow the guidance.

Developing intuitive capacity also involves creating regular quiet time where your nervous system can calm down enough for subtle signals to become noticeable. This doesn't require formal meditation or elaborate spiritual practices, but it does mean building brief periods of stillness into your daily routine where you're not consuming information, solving problems, or managing tasks.

These quiet moments might happen while drinking your morning coffee before checking your phone, taking a few deep breaths before entering meetings, or spending a few minutes in your car before going into your house at the end of the day. The goal is creating space where your mind can settle and your attention can turn inward long enough to notice what your inner guidance system wants you to know about your current situation or upcoming choices.

Journaling can also support intuitive development by giving you a way to explore hunches and gut feelings without committing to major actions based on incomplete guidance. You might write about what your intuition seems to be telling you about a relationship, career decision, or life direction, then notice how those insights develop and clarify over time. This process helps you learn to distinguish between wishful thinking and genuine guidance while building confidence in your ability to receive and interpret your inner voice.

The reconnection process requires patience because intuitive capacity develops gradually through consistent attention rather than sudden break-through experiences. Most people notice small improvements in their ability to sense what feels right within a few weeks of regular practice, but developing reliable trust in inner guidance typically takes several months of learning to distinguish between mental noise and authentic signals.

Working with small, low-risk decisions provides excellent practice for developing intuitive skills without major consequences if your guidance turns out to be inaccurate. You might use gut feelings to choose which route to take to work, what to order at restaurants, or which friend to call when you want company. These everyday choices give you opportunities to practice accessing and following your inner voice while building a track record that helps you learn when your guidance tends to be most reliable.

The goal is not to replace analytical thinking with intuitive decision-making but to integrate both sources of wisdom so you can access whichever type of guidance is most appropriate for different situations. Complex financial decisions might require careful analysis, while choices about relationships and creative projects might benefit more from intuitive insight.

Learning when to lead with logic versus when to trust your gut becomes part of developing mature decision-making capacity.

Setting Intentions That Work

Most intention-setting practices fail because they focus on what you think you should want rather than what you authentically desire, creating goals that look good on paper but don't generate the emotional energy needed to sustain effort over time. When your intentions emerge from social expectations, family pressure, or mental ideas about success rather than genuine inner calling, you end up working toward outcomes that feel empty even when you achieve them.

Effective intention-setting requires learning to distinguish between ego-driven goals that promise external validation or security and soul-level desires that emerge from your authentic self and deeper values. Ego-based intentions often involve comparing yourself to others, seeking approval or recognition, or trying to fix perceived inadequacies through achievement. These goals might motivate short-term effort, but they rarely create lasting satisfaction because they're based on external measures rather than internal alignment.

Soul-level intentions feel different in your body because they generate genuine excitement, curiosity, or a sense of rightness rather than pressure, anxiety, or obligation. When you consider pursuing something that truly aligns with your authentic desires, you typically feel energized and expanded rather than contracted and stressed. Your nervous system recognizes the difference between moving toward what you genuinely want versus what you think you should want.

The process of discovering authentic intentions begins with creating space to explore what you actually care about rather than what you've been told to value or what would impress other people. This exploration requires honest self-reflection about what brings you joy, what problems you feel called to solve, what experiences you crave, and what kind of person you want to become, independent of external expectations or social approval.

Asking yourself quality questions can help clarify authentic desires that might be buried under layers of conditioning and obligation. What would you pursue if you knew you couldn't fail? What activities make you lose track of time because you enjoy them so much? What injustices or problems make you feel angry or passionate about creating change? What kind of legacy do you want to leave through how you lived and what you contributed?

These questions bypass rational analysis and connect you directly with emotional and intuitive responses that reveal what matters most to you at a deeper level. The answers might surprise you because they often differ significantly from the goals you've been pursuing based on logical reasoning about what would be practical, profitable, or socially acceptable.

Effective intentions also need to be specific enough to guide action but flexible enough to allow for unexpected opportunities and changing circumstances. Instead of rigid goals with detailed timelines and exact outcomes, intuitive intentions provide direction and focus while remaining open to how that direction might unfold in your actual life experience.

For example, instead of setting a goal to "get promoted to senior manager within two years," you might set an intention to "develop my leadership skills and find opportunities to make a bigger impact through my work." The first goal locks you into a specific outcome that might not be available or might not serve you when the time comes. The second intention gives you direction while allowing for multiple ways that leadership development and increased impact could manifest.

This flexibility is crucial because life rarely unfolds according to detailed plans, and rigid goals often prevent you from recognizing better opportunities that don't match your original expectations. Intuitive intentions work with the unpredictability of life rather than against it, helping you stay aligned with your deeper purposes while remaining open to unexpected possibilities.

Energy-based intention-setting involves paying attention to how different possibilities feel in your body rather than only considering them intellectually. When you imagine pursuing various directions, notice which ones generate excitement, curiosity, or a sense of expansion and which ones feel heavy, draining, or constrictive. Your nervous system often knows which choices would serve you before your rational mind can analyze all the factors involved.

This body-based assessment becomes particularly valuable when you're choosing between options that all seem reasonable from a logical perspective. Your analytical mind might struggle to decide between job offers that have similar benefits and drawbacks, but your intuitive sense might clearly prefer one opportunity because it feels more aligned with your authentic interests and values.

Seasonal intention-setting recognizes that your authentic desires and energy levels change throughout the year, and what feels right in January might not align with who you've become by June. Instead of creating annual resolutions that you're supposed to maintain regardless of changing circumstances, you can set intentions quarterly or even monthly based on what feels most important and energizing in your current life situation.

This approach prevents the common problem of abandoning intentions entirely when they stop feeling relevant rather than updating them to match your evolving priorities and circumstances. Life is dynamic, and your intentions can be dynamic too, providing ongoing guidance that stays connected to your authentic desires rather than becoming obligations you drag along out of habit.

Intention-setting also benefits from including both external goals and internal qualities you want to develop. While it's important to pursue meaningful achievements and experiences, focusing only on external outcomes can create attachment and anxiety that interfere with enjoying the journey toward your goals. Balancing external intentions with internal ones helps you grow as a person regardless of whether specific outcomes manifest as expected.

Internal intentions might include developing patience, courage, creativity, or compassion while you're working toward external goals like career advancement, relationship improvements, or health changes. These character-based intentions ensure that you're becoming the kind of person you want to be while you're pursuing the experiences and achievements you desire, creating fulfillment that doesn't depend entirely on external circumstances.

The most powerful intentions often involve service to others or contribution to something larger than your personal interests because these purposes provide meaning that sustains motivation even when the work becomes difficult or progress feels slow. When your intentions include making a positive difference in other people's lives or addressing problems you care about, you tap into sources of energy and commitment that purely self-focused goals rarely generate.

This doesn't mean abandoning personal desires in favor of sacrifice or martyrdom, but rather finding ways that your authentic interests and abilities can serve purposes that extend beyond your immediate needs. When your personal fulfillment and contribution to others align, you access sustainable motivation that feels energizing rather than depleting over time.

The Daily Intuition Integration Practice

Building reliable access to your inner voice requires consistent daily practice that gradually trains your nervous system to recognize and trust intuitive signals rather than only relying on mental analysis for guidance. This integration happens through small, regular interactions with your intuitive capacity that build confidence and skill over time, rather than dramatic breakthrough experiences that might feel inspiring but don't create lasting change in how you make decisions.

The foundation practice involves pausing before decisions to check in with your gut feeling, regardless of how small or insignificant the choice might seem. This could happen when you're deciding what to wear, which route to take to work, what to order for lunch, or how to respond to an email. The goal is not to make intuition-based choices in every situation but to develop the habit of consulting your inner voice as one source of information alongside logical analysis.

These decision-point pauses only need to last ten to fifteen seconds, just long enough to notice what your body and emotions are telling you about the options you're considering. You might ask yourself simple questions like "What feels right here?" or "What does my gut say about this?" or "Which choice feels more aligned with who I want to be?" The answers don't always need to override rational considerations, but they provide additional information that can improve the quality of your decisions.

Morning intention-setting creates a daily practice for connecting with your authentic desires rather than just moving through your schedule on autopilot. Instead of immediately checking your phone or jumping into tasks, you spend a few minutes asking your inner guidance system what it wants you to know about the day ahead, what deserves your attention and energy, and how you want to show up in your various roles and relationships.

This morning check-in helps you approach your day from intention rather than reaction, making choices throughout the day that align with your deeper values rather than just responding to immediate pressures and demands. You might discover that your intuition wants you to prioritize a conversation you've been avoiding, to spend extra time on a project that excites you, or to take care of your energy levels so you can be present for evening family time.

Body awareness practices throughout the day help you notice the physical signals that carry intuitive information about your environment, relationships, and decisions. This might involve checking in with your breathing, posture, and muscle tension periodically to notice whether you feel relaxed and open or stressed and contracted in different situations.

These body check-ins become particularly valuable during interactions with other people because your nervous system often picks up on dynamics and energy that your conscious mind processes more slowly. You might notice that your shoulders tense during conversations with certain colleagues, that your chest feels open and warm when you're with specific friends, or that your stomach churns when someone is being dishonest, even if their words sound convincing.

Evening reflection provides daily practice for recognizing when you followed your inner guidance and when you overrode it, helping you learn to distinguish between authentic intuitive signals and mental noise or emotional reactivity. You might ask yourself questions like "When did

I trust my gut today and how did that work out?" or "Were there moments when I ignored my inner voice and what happened as a result?"

This reflection builds self-awareness about your patterns and helps you recognize the difference between fear-based reactions and wisdom-based responses. Over time, you'll notice that following authentic inner guidance typically leads to better outcomes and more satisfaction than making decisions based only on logical analysis or social expectations.

The integration practice also includes experimenting with small, low-risk actions based on intuitive impulses to build confidence in your ability to receive and act on inner guidance. This might involve calling someone who's been on your mind, taking a different route home because it feels right, or pursuing a creative project that excites you even if you can't explain why it appeals to you.

These experiments provide opportunities to practice trusting your intuition without major consequences if the guidance turns out to be inaccurate or incomplete. When you follow small intuitive impulses and get positive results, you build confidence that supports trusting your inner voice in more significant situations. When the results are neutral or negative, you gain information about how your guidance system works and when it tends to be most reliable.

Distinguishing between mental chatter and authentic inner guidance becomes easier with practice as you learn to recognize the different qualities of these two types of internal communication. Mental chatter tends to be repetitive, anxious, and focused on problems or what could go wrong. Authentic intuition usually feels calm, clear, and focused on what would serve your highest good, even when it's pointing toward challenging or uncertain choices.

Intuitive guidance also tends to arrive complete rather than building up through analysis, and it often includes information about timing and approach that pure logic might miss. Your inner voice might tell you not only what to do but when to do it and how to approach the situation in ways that honor everyone involved.

Weekly intuition reviews help you track patterns in when your inner guidance is most accessible and accurate, allowing you to optimize conditions for receiving clear signals when you need them most. You might notice that your intuition is clearest in the morning before mental activity gets busy, or that you receive better guidance when you're well-rested and not stressed, or that certain environments or activities help you access inner guidance more easily.

This self-knowledge allows you to create optimal conditions for important decision-making rather than trying to access intuitive guidance when your system is overwhelmed or distracted. You might schedule important choices for times when your inner voice tends to be most available, or use specific practices that help you calm down and tune in when you need guidance about complex situations.

The ultimate goal of daily integration is for checking in with your intuition to become as automatic as looking both ways before crossing the street. You want to develop the habit of consulting your inner voice naturally rather than only remembering to do it during designated practice times or when you're facing major decisions. This requires consistent practice with small choices until accessing intuitive guidance becomes a normal part of how you navigate daily life.

Intuitive Intention Implementation Process

Reconnecting with your intuitive guidance system requires understanding that the disconnection happened through years of conditioning that prioritized analytical thinking over inner knowing, not because your guidance system is fundamentally flawed or unreliable. Your body constantly receives information through physical sensations, emotional responses, and sudden knowing that can inform better decisions when you learn to recognize and trust these signals alongside logical analysis rather than instead of it.

Effective intention-setting emerges from authentic desires that generate genuine energy and excitement rather than goals based on what you think you should want or what would impress others. When your intentions align with your deeper values and authentic interests, pursuing them feels energizing rather than draining because you're moving toward what you genuinely care about rather than what external expectations demand.

Your first implementation step is to establish decision-point pauses before three small choices you make every day, such as what to wear, which route to take somewhere, or what to eat for lunch. Before making these decisions, pause for ten to fifteen seconds to ask "What feels right here?" or "What does my gut say about this?" Notice any physical sensations, emotional responses, or sudden knowing that emerges, and use this information alongside logical considerations.

The goal is not to make purely intuitive choices but to develop the habit of consulting your inner voice as one valuable source of information. Some decisions will benefit more from analytical thinking, while others will be improved by trusting gut feelings. Learning when to lead with logic versus when to trust intuition becomes part of developing mature decision-making capacity.

Your second step is to create a brief morning intention-setting practice where you spend three to five minutes asking your inner voice what it wants you to know about the day ahead. Instead of immediately checking your phone or jumping into tasks, pause to sense what deserves your attention and energy, how you want to show up in your various roles, and what would feel most aligned with your authentic desires.

Write down any insights or guidance that emerges, not as rigid plans you must follow but as direction that can inform your choices throughout the day. This practice helps you approach daily activities from intention rather than reaction, making decisions that align with your deeper values rather than just responding to immediate pressures.

Your third step is to practice body awareness check-ins three times throughout your day by pausing to notice your breathing, posture, and muscle tension. Ask yourself whether you feel relaxed and open or stressed and contracted, especially during interactions with other people or when considering different options. Your nervous system often picks up on dynamics and information that your conscious mind processes more slowly.

Pay particular attention to how your body responds to different people, environments, and choices. Notice if your shoulders tense with certain colleagues, if your chest feels warm and open with specific friends, or if your stomach churns when someone is being dishonest. These physical signals carry valuable information about your circumstances that can inform better decisions when you learn to recognize and trust them.

Your fourth step is to experiment with one small, low-risk action based on an intuitive impulse each day for the next week. This might involve calling someone who's been on your mind, taking a different route because it feels right, or spending time on a creative project that excites you even if you can't explain logically why it appeals to you. These experiments build confidence in your ability to receive and act on inner guidance without major consequences if the results aren't perfect.

Track what happens when you follow these small intuitive impulses versus when you override them in favor of purely logical choices. Notice whether trusting your gut feelings generally leads to better outcomes, more satisfaction, or unexpected opportunities that wouldn't have been available through analytical decision-making alone.

Your final step is to establish an evening reflection practice where you spend two to three minutes asking yourself when you trusted your inner guidance during the day and when you overrode it. Notice the difference between fear-based mental chatter and authentic intuitive signals, and observe how following your inner voice typically affects your energy levels, relationships, and overall satisfaction with your choices.

Use your daily tracking question **"Did I check in with my intuition before at least one decision today?"** to build consistency with consulting your inner voice rather than only relying on mental analysis. This yes-or-no tracking focuses on the practice of accessing intuitive guidance rather than the quality of the insights you receive, building the habit that allows your inner voice to become increasingly clear and reliable over time.

6

F is for FAMILY and FRIENDS

Does this sound familiar? Your phone buzzes with another text message while you're having dinner with your family. You glance at it automatically, even though you promised yourself you'd be present tonight. Your teenager barely looks up from their own device, your partner scrolls through social media between bites, and the conversation stays safely on surface topics like schedules and logistics. Everyone is physically present, but no one is really here.

This scene plays out in millions of homes every day, reflecting a quiet crisis that's stealing the joy and connection from our most important relationships. You're busier than ever, more connected through technology than any generation in history, yet somehow lonelier and more disconnected from the people who matter most. The relationships that should nourish your soul have become another set of obligations to manage rather than sources of energy and meaning.

You know your relationships need attention, but finding time for meaningful connection feels impossible when everyone's schedules are packed with work, school, activities, and endless digital distractions. The conversations you do have stay focused on practical matters because deeper topics feel too time-consuming or emotionally risky when you're already stretched thin. You end up maintaining relationships rather than truly enjoying them.

The cost of this surface-level relating is high. It shows up as a persistent loneliness that exists even when you're surrounded by people, a sense that no one really knows who you are beneath your various roles and responsibilities, and the gradual erosion of the emotional intimacy that makes relationships feel worthwhile rather than burdensome. This chapter will show you how to transform obligatory interactions into soul-deep connections that energize rather than drain you.

The Connection Crisis

The modern relationship crisis isn't dramatic or obvious like divorce or family feuds, but it's equally destructive to your wellbeing and happiness. It's the slow drift toward surface-level interactions that maintain the appearance of connection while leaving everyone feeling unseen and unknown. You might spend hours each day with family members or talk regularly with close friends, yet feel like you're going through the motions of a relationship rather than experiencing genuine intimacy and understanding.

This drift happens gradually and often goes unnoticed because everyone involved adapts to increasingly shallow interactions without recognizing what's being lost. Conversations become focused on logistics, schedules, and problem-solving rather than sharing thoughts, feelings, and experiences that reveal who you really are. You discuss what needs to happen, but rarely explore what you're thinking about, what's exciting you, what's worrying you, or what you're learning about yourself and life.

The busyness that characterizes most people's lives creates conditions where superficial relating feels necessary for efficiency. When you have limited time together, it seems practical to focus on coordinating schedules, making decisions, and handling responsibilities rather than having leisurely conversations about ideas, dreams, or emotional experiences. But this practical approach gradually erodes the emotional intimacy that makes relationships feel meaningful rather than functional.

Technology amplifies this problem by creating the illusion of connection through frequent but shallow digital interactions. You might text with family members throughout the day, follow friends on social media, and feel like you're staying connected, but these interactions rarely involve the vulnerability and presence that create genuine intimacy. You know what people are doing but not how they're feeling about their experiences or what those experiences mean to them.

The result is relationships that feel obligatory rather than joyful, draining rather than energizing, and isolated rather than connected. You maintain contact and fulfill your relational duties, but you miss the deeper satisfaction that comes from being truly known and accepted by the people you love. This emotional distance creates a loneliness that persists even when you're surrounded by family and friends because surface-level interactions don't address your fundamental need to be seen and understood.

The crisis becomes particularly painful when you realize that years have passed without having meaningful conversations with people you care about most. Your relationships exist in a kind of emotional maintenance mode where you handle practical matters and share basic information, but you don't really know what your teenager is thinking about beyond school and activities, what your partner dreams about beyond immediate goals and concerns, or what your close friends are learning about themselves through their life experiences.

This lack of deeper knowing creates relationships that feel fragile and disconnected from your authentic self. When no one really understands who you are beneath your roles and responsibilities, you carry the burden of your inner life alone. Your thoughts, insights, struggles, and growth remain private, creating isolation that undermines your sense of belonging and acceptance even within your closest relationships.

The emotional distance also affects your capacity for joy and celebration because surface-level relationships can't fully appreciate your achievements, growth, and positive experiences. When people don't understand your deeper values, interests, and aspirations, they can't celebrate your successes in ways that feel truly meaningful or provide support during challenges in ways that address your actual needs rather than what they assume you need.

Children particularly suffer from this connection crisis because they're developing their sense of self and their capacity for intimacy through their family relationships. When family interactions focus primarily on behavior management, academic performance, and activity coordination, children don't learn how to share their inner world or how to be curious about other people's emotional experiences. They adapt to surface-level relating as normal, carrying these patterns into their future relationships.

The crisis also perpetuates itself because people lose practice with emotional intimacy and vulnerability, making deeper conversations feel awkward or risky when they do attempt them. When you're accustomed to discussing practical matters and avoiding emotional topics, sharing feelings and personal insights feels uncomfortable and unfamiliar. The skills for creating and maintaining emotional intimacy atrophy from lack of use.

Recognizing this connection crisis is the first step toward addressing it, but the solution requires intentional changes in how you approach your relationships rather than hoping that a deeper connection will happen naturally when life gets less busy. The crisis didn't develop because you don't care about the people in your life; it developed because the conditions of modern living work against the presence and vulnerability that intimate relationships require.

The good news is that even small changes in how you interact with family and friends can begin to restore emotional intimacy and genuine connection. People are hungry for deeper relationships and typically respond positively when someone creates opportunities for more meaningful interaction. The challenge is learning how to create these opportunities within the constraints of busy schedules and established patterns of surface-level relating.

The Presence Practice

Presence is the foundation that transforms ordinary interactions into moments of genuine connection, but most people have lost the ability to be fully present with others because their attention is constantly divided between multiple sources of stimulation and concern. True presence means bringing your complete attention to the person in front of you, setting aside your mental to-do list, your phone, and your preoccupation with other matters to create space where real intimacy can emerge.

The practice begins with recognizing how rarely you give anyone your undivided attention, even during conversations that seem important or meaningful. Your mind typically operates on multiple tracks simultaneously, listening to what someone is saying while also thinking about your response, planning what you need to do next, or processing information from your environment. This divided attention prevents the deep listening that allows people to feel truly heard and understood.

Learning to be present starts with simple awareness of when your attention drifts away from the person you're with and gently bringing it back without judgment or self-criticism. This happens constantly for everyone, so the goal is not perfect attention but increased awareness of your attention patterns and more frequent returns to presence when you notice you've drifted away.

Physical presence supports emotional and mental presence by creating conditions where focused attention becomes easier to maintain. This means putting away phones and other devices during conversations, turning your body toward the person you're talking with, making eye contact when culturally appropriate, and eliminating distractions from your immediate environment when possible.

These physical adjustments signal to both you and the other person that this interaction matters enough to deserve full attention. When you continue checking your phone or handling other tasks while someone is talking, you communicate that they're not important enough to warrant your complete focus, even if you don't intend to send that message.

Emotional presence involves setting aside your own agenda, judgments, and desire to fix or change the other person so you can simply receive what they're sharing with you. Most conversations involve people waiting for their turn to talk rather than truly listening to understand the other person's experience. When you're formulating your response while someone is speaking, you're not fully present to what they're actually saying.

This agenda-free listening allows people to feel heard in ways they rarely experience, even in close relationships. When someone shares something with you and you respond with curiosity and acceptance rather than advice, criticism, or your own similar experience, they feel seen and valued for who they are rather than evaluated for how well they're handling their life.

The practice of reflecting back what you hear helps maintain presence while showing the other person that you're truly paying attention to their experience. This doesn't mean parroting their words but rather acknowledging the emotions and meaning you're picking up from what they're sharing. You might say something like "It sounds like you're feeling frustrated about the situation at work" or "I hear how excited you are about this new opportunity."

This reflection serves multiple purposes: it keeps you focused on understanding rather than preparing your response, it gives the other person confirmation that they're being heard accurately, and it creates space for them to go deeper into their experience rather than moving quickly to the next topic. Most people rarely feel truly understood, so this simple practice can transform the quality of your relationships.

Presence also involves tolerating silence and emotional intensity rather than rushing to fill gaps in conversation or smooth over difficult feelings. When someone is processing emotions or trying to articulate something important, they need space and time rather than immediate responses or solutions. Learning to sit comfortably with pauses and strong emotions allows deeper sharing to emerge.

This comfort with intensity and silence develops gradually as you practice staying present during conversations that involve difficult topics or strong feelings. Instead of immediately trying to make someone feel better or moving to lighter subjects, you learn to stay with whatever is emerging and trust that your presence itself is helpful and healing.

Curiosity becomes a powerful tool for maintaining presence because it keeps you focused on understanding the other person's experience rather than judging it or trying to change it. When someone shares something that surprises, concerns, or confuses you, responding with genuine questions about their perspective keeps you present and engaged rather than reactive or defensive.

This curious approach might involve asking questions like "What was that experience like for you?" or "How are you feeling about that situation?" or "What's most important to you as you think about this decision?" These questions invite deeper sharing while showing that you're interested in understanding their inner world rather than just the external facts of their situation.

The presence practice also includes being willing to share your own authentic thoughts and feelings rather than only listening to others. Genuine intimacy requires vulnerability from both people, so learning to reveal your inner experience appropriately creates opportunities for others to know and understand you more deeply. This vulnerability needs to be balanced and reciprocal rather than one-sided sharing that overwhelms the other person.

Regular presence practice with family and friends gradually changes the entire dynamic of your relationships because people begin to associate spending time with you with feeling heard, understood, and valued. They start bringing their real concerns and experiences to you rather than only discussing surface-level topics because they trust that you'll receive what they share with acceptance and genuine interest.

The transformation happens slowly but becomes increasingly noticeable as conversations naturally go deeper, emotional intimacy increases, and people feel more comfortable being authentic in your presence. What started as a practice of paying better attention evolves into relationships that feel nourishing and meaningful rather than obligatory and draining.

Healing Relationships

Relationships that have become strained or superficial can be gradually warmed and deepened through specific approaches that rebuild trust and intimacy without forcing vulnerability or creating pressure for immediate transformation. The healing process requires patience, consistency, and willingness to take responsibility for your part in the distance without demanding that the other person change their behavior or attitude at the same pace you're changing yours.

The first step involves an honest assessment of how the relationship became distant, focusing on patterns and circumstances rather than blame or fault-finding. Most relationship cooling happens gradually through accumulated small disconnections rather than major conflicts or betrayals. You might have stopped asking meaningful questions, sharing personal experiences, or making time for unhurried conversations. The other person might have done the same, creating a cycle of increasing superficiality.

Understanding these patterns helps you identify specific changes you can make without requiring the other person to acknowledge problems or commit to working on the relationship. You can begin asking better questions, sharing more authentically, and creating opportunities for deeper connection, regardless of whether they initially respond with matching vulnerability or engagement.

Starting with appreciation and acknowledgment of positive qualities creates emotional safety that makes people more receptive to increased intimacy and connection. When relationships have grown cold, people often focus on what's wrong or missing rather than what's still good and valuable. Beginning your healing efforts by expressing genuine gratitude for who they are and what they contribute to your life helps rebuild the foundation of positive regard that supports deeper intimacy.

This appreciation needs to be specific and authentic rather than generic compliments or obvious attempts to manipulate their feelings. Notice and acknowledge particular qualities, actions, or contributions that you genuinely value, and express this appreciation in ways that feel natural rather than forced or therapeutic. The goal is to remind both of you why this relationship matters and what's worth preserving and developing.

Gentle curiosity about their inner world helps rebuild intimacy without creating pressure for immediate deep sharing. Instead of asking invasive questions or pushing for emotional conversations, you can show interest in their thoughts, feelings, and experiences through casual but genuine inquiry. This might involve asking how they're feeling about changes at work, what they're enjoying about their hobbies, or what they're thinking about regarding family situations.

These questions need to come from authentic interest rather than a relationship repair agenda, and you need to be prepared to receive whatever level of sharing they're comfortable with rather than pushing for more vulnerability than they're ready to offer. Some people will respond immediately to increased interest, while others need time to trust that your curiosity is genuine and safe.

Creating opportunities for shared positive experiences helps rebuild the emotional connection that supports deeper intimacy. When relationships have become focused on problems, logistics, and obligations, people associate spending time together with stress and conflict rather than enjoyment and connection. Intentionally creating pleasant experiences together reminds everyone why they care about each other and want to invest in the relationship.

These shared experiences don't need to be elaborate or expensive, but they should involve activities that both people enjoy and that create natural opportunities for conversation and connection. This might involve cooking meals together, taking walks, attending events you both find interesting, or engaging in hobbies that allow for relaxed interaction while doing something enjoyable.

Addressing past hurts or conflicts may be necessary for some relationships, but this should happen after you've rebuilt some positive connection rather than as the first step in the healing process. When relationships are already strained, immediately focusing on problems and grievances often makes the distance worse rather than better. Building positive momentum first creates the emotional resources needed to handle difficult conversations constructively.

When you do need to address past issues, focus on your own experience and feelings rather than criticizing their behavior or demanding apologies. Use "I" statements to share how certain situations affected you while acknowledging your own contributions to relationship problems. This approach invites dialogue rather than defensiveness and creates opportunities for mutual understanding rather than blame and counter-blame.

Consistency over intensity proves more effective for healing distant relationships than dramatic gestures or intense conversations that might feel overwhelming or manipulative. Small, regular efforts to connect and show care build trust gradually and feel sustainable for both people. A brief weekly phone call, a thoughtful text message, or a small gesture of consideration demonstrates ongoing commitment without creating pressure for immediate reciprocation.

This consistent approach also allows you to maintain your healing efforts even when the other person doesn't respond immediately or positively. Some people need time to trust that changes in your behavior are genuine and lasting rather than temporary attempts to get something from them. Your consistency demonstrates that you value the relationship enough to invest in it regardless of immediate returns.

Setting appropriate boundaries protects your emotional wellbeing while you're working to heal relationships, especially when the other person responds to your efforts with continued coldness, criticism, or rejection. You can continue offering warmth and connection without allowing yourself to be mistreated or taken advantage of. This might involve limiting contact if interactions consistently leave you feeling worse, or maintaining your caring approach while not tolerating disrespectful behavior.

These boundaries help you sustain your healing efforts over time rather than burning out from giving more than you can afford emotionally. They also model healthy relationship dynamics that can eventually improve how the other person treats you, even if that's not your primary motivation for maintaining boundaries.

Accepting that some relationships may not heal despite your best efforts allows you to invest energy wisely while maintaining realistic expectations. Not everyone is capable of or interested in deeper intimacy, and some relationship damage is too extensive to repair through individual effort alone. Recognizing these limitations helps you decide how much energy to invest and when to focus your attention on relationships that are more responsive to your healing efforts.

This acceptance doesn't mean giving up prematurely or becoming cynical about relationship possibilities, but rather maintaining realistic expectations while continuing to offer what you can without depleting yourself. Sometimes your consistent loving approach plants seeds that don't bloom until years later, and sometimes it simply allows you to feel good about how you handled a difficult relationship situation.

Creating Rituals and Traditions

Meaningful traditions and rituals create consistent opportunities for connection that don't depend on anyone remembering to prioritize relationships when life gets busy, but most attempts to establish new family practices fail because they're too elaborate, time-consuming, or disconnected from your family's actual interests and schedule constraints. Successful traditions work with your real life rather than requiring you to become different people with more time and energy than you actually have.

The key to creating sustainable traditions lies in building on activities and moments that already exist in your routine rather than adding entirely new obligations to everyone's schedule. Instead of trying to institute weekly family game nights that require clearing everyone's calendar, you might create a tradition around meals you're already sharing, car rides you're already taking, or bedtime routines that already happen regularly.

These existing moments provide natural opportunities for deeper connection without requiring additional time commitments that compete with work, school, and other obligations. When you enhance activities that are already happening rather than creating new ones, you're more likely to maintain the tradition consistently because it doesn't feel like another item on an already overwhelming to-do list.

Starting small and simple increases the likelihood that new traditions will actually stick rather than being abandoned when initial enthusiasm fades. A tradition of sharing one highlight from each person's day during dinner takes five minutes and requires no preparation or special materials. A practice of taking a brief walk together after family meals provides connection time while supporting everyone's health and wellbeing.

These simple traditions can evolve and expand over time as they become established parts of your routine, but starting with elaborate plans often leads to failure when the reality of maintaining complex practices becomes overwhelming. It's better to consistently do something small and meaningful than to occasionally do something elaborate that can't be sustained long-term.

Involving everyone in choosing and designing traditions increases buy-in and ensures that the practices actually appeal to the people who will be participating in them. Instead of unilaterally deciding what your family or friend group should do together, have conversations about what kinds of activities everyone enjoys and what times work best for regular connection.

This collaborative approach helps you discover preferences and constraints you might not have considered, and it gives everyone ownership in the tradition rather than making them feel like they're complying with someone else's agenda. When people help create the practices, they're more likely to participate willingly and suggest improvements that make the traditions more enjoyable for everyone.

Flexibility within structure allows traditions to adapt to changing circumstances and preferences while maintaining their essential purpose of creating regular connection. Instead of rigid rules about exactly what must happen and when, establish the core intention of spending meaningful time together and allow the specific activities to vary based on seasons, schedules, and interests.

For example, a tradition of "adventure Saturdays" might involve hiking in good weather, visiting museums when it's raining, cooking special meals during busy periods, or having movie marathons when people need to rest. The consistency comes from the commitment to spending focused time together, not from doing identical activities every time.

Seasonal traditions work particularly well because they align with natural rhythms and provide anticipation and structure throughout the year without requiring weekly or daily maintenance. Annual traditions like special birthday celebrations, holiday customs, or summer activities create family identity and shared memories while being manageable to maintain over time.

These seasonal practices might include camping trips, holiday baking, spring cleaning projects done together, or back-to-school shopping traditions. The key is choosing activities that feel celebratory and meaningful rather than obligatory, and that create opportunities for conversation and connection while accomplishing the seasonal activity.

Friend traditions require different approaches than family rituals because friendships involve more scheduling complexity and less built-in time together, but they're equally important for maintaining close relationships over time. Successful friend traditions often involve regular but not frequent commitments that provide a consistent connection without overwhelming busy schedules.

This might involve monthly dinners, quarterly weekend activities, annual trips or celebrations, or weekly phone calls with long-distance friends. The specific activity matters less than the commitment to regular connection and the understanding that these relationships deserve intentional time and attention rather than only getting together when it's convenient.

Technology can support friend traditions when geographic distance or scheduling challenges make in-person connection difficult, but the key is using technology to enhance real relationships rather than substituting digital interaction for meaningful connection. Regular video calls, online book clubs, or shared digital projects can maintain intimacy when physical presence isn't possible.

The most effective digital friend traditions involve real-time interaction and shared experiences rather than just exchanging messages or social media updates. Watching movies together online, playing games, or having structured conversations about meaningful topics creates a connection that feels more substantial than casual texting or posting updates.

Celebrating and acknowledging the traditions as they develop helps reinforce their importance and creates positive associations that motivate continued participation. Taking photos, keeping journals, or simply expressing appreciation for the connection these practices create helps everyone recognize their value and feel motivated to maintain them over time.

When everyone feels ownership in the tradition and sees its positive effects on relationships, they become partners in maintaining and developing the practice rather than passive participants who might lose interest over time.

Recovering from lapses in traditions without abandoning them entirely requires treating missed occasions as temporary interruptions rather than permanent failures. Life circumstances, busy periods, and changing priorities will inevitably interfere with even the best-intentioned traditions, but these interruptions don't need to end the practice permanently.

When you notice that a tradition has been neglected, simply restart it without elaborate explanations or guilt about the gap. Acknowledge that life got busy and express enthusiasm about reconnecting through your established practice. This approach models resilience and commitment while avoiding the all-or-nothing thinking that leads people to abandon traditions entirely after missing them a few times.

Family and Friends Implementation Process

The connection crisis affecting most relationships stems from the gradual drift toward surface-level interactions that maintain the appearance of connection while leaving everyone feeling unseen and unknown. This crisis develops through busyness, digital distractions, and the practical focus that seems necessary for managing complex lives, but it can be reversed through intentional presence practices and the creation of meaningful traditions that provide consistent opportunities for deeper connection.

Presence transforms ordinary interactions into moments of genuine intimacy by bringing complete attention to the person in front of you, setting aside distractions and agendas to create space where authentic sharing can emerge. Healing distant relationships requires patience, consistency, and willingness to rebuild trust through appreciation, gentle curiosity, and shared positive experiences rather than immediately addressing problems or demanding vulnerability.

Your first implementation step is to practice presence during one conversation each day by eliminating distractions and bringing your complete attention to the person you're talking with. Put away your phone, turn your body toward them, make eye contact when appropriate, and focus on understanding their experience rather than preparing your response or thinking about other matters.

When you notice your attention drifting to other concerns, gently bring it back to the person in front of you without judging yourself for the distraction. Practice reflecting back what you hear by acknowledging the emotions and meaning you're picking up from what they're sharing, using phrases like "It sounds like you're feeling…" or "I hear how important this is to you."

Your second step is to identify one relationship that has grown distant or superficial and begin the healing process by expressing specific appreciation for who that person is and what they contribute to your life. Notice and acknowledge particular qualities, actions, or contributions that you genuinely value, and share this appreciation in ways that feel natural rather than forced or therapeutic.

Follow this appreciation with gentle curiosity about their inner world by asking questions about their thoughts, feelings, and experiences rather than only discussing practical matters. Show authentic interest in how they're feeling about work changes, what they're enjoying about their hobbies, or what they're thinking about regarding family situations. Be prepared to receive whatever level of sharing they're comfortable with, rather than pushing for more vulnerability than they're ready to offer.

Your third step is to create one simple, sustainable tradition with your family or a close friend that builds on activities or moments that already exist in your routine rather than adding entirely new obligations to everyone's schedule. This might involve sharing highlights from each person's day during meals you're already eating together, taking brief walks after dinner, or having weekly phone calls with friends who live far away.

Start small and simple to increase the likelihood that the tradition will actually stick rather than being abandoned when initial enthusiasm fades. A five-minute practice that happens consistently will create more connection over time than an elaborate tradition that only happens occasionally when everyone has extra time and energy.

Your fourth step is to establish a weekly relationship review where you reflect on the quality of your connections with family and friends during the past seven days. Ask yourself which relationships received meaningful attention, which interactions felt genuinely connected versus superficial, and what opportunities you might have missed for deeper connection.

Use this review to identify patterns in when and how you create meaningful connections versus when you default to surface-level relating. Notice whether you're more present during certain times of day, in specific environments, or with particular people, and use this information to optimize conditions for deeper relationship experiences.

Your final step is to practice one act of relationship generosity each day by doing something that demonstrates care and attention for someone you love without expecting anything in return. This might involve sending an encouraging text message, preparing someone's favorite snack, offering help with a task they're struggling with, or simply listening without giving advice when they need to process something difficult.

These acts of generosity build positive momentum in your relationships while demonstrating that you value the people in your life enough to invest time and energy in their wellbeing.

Track your relationship focus using the daily question **"Did I have a meaningful connection with someone I care about today?"** focusing on quality of interaction rather than quantity of contact.

The goal is to transform your relationships from obligations you manage into sources of energy and meaning that nourish your soul while providing the same gift of authentic connection to the people you love. When relationships become soul-deep rather than surface-level, they support and enhance all other areas of personal growth rather than competing with them for your limited time and attention.

7

T is for TREASURED WISDOM

Your bookshelf tells a story you know by heart. Row after row of personal development books, some with pristine spines that have never been cracked, others with highlighted pages and folded corners marking profound insights you were certain would change your life. You've attended workshops where speakers shared wisdom that felt revolutionary in the moment, had conversations with mentors whose advice seemed like the missing piece you'd been searching for, and experienced breakthrough moments where everything suddenly made perfect sense.

Yet here you are, months or years later, facing the same challenges and making the same mistakes despite having collected enough wisdom to transform a dozen lives. The insights that felt so powerful when you first encountered them have faded into background noise, competing with new information and daily distractions until they become just more items in your mental library of good ideas you don't actually use.

This isn't because the wisdom was wrong or because you lack the intelligence to apply it. The problem lies in treating wisdom like information to be consumed rather than truth to be lived, collecting insights like trophies rather than integrating them into the fabric of your daily experience until they become automatic responses rather than conscious efforts.

The difference between collecting and living wisdom determines whether your learning creates lasting transformation or just makes you a more

91

knowledgeable person who continues operating from the same patterns that brought you to seek wisdom in the first place. This chapter will show you how to bridge that gap through systematic integration practices that turn the insights you've already gathered into the principles that guide your decisions and shape your character.

Consumption Pattern

The endless accumulation of wisdom without application has become a sophisticated form of procrastination that keeps you busy learning instead of actually changing, creating the illusion of progress while maintaining familiar patterns that feel safe even when they don't serve you. Every new book you buy, workshop you attend, or insight you collect provides a temporary sense of forward movement that satisfies your desire for growth without requiring the discomfort of actually implementing what you learn.

This consumption pattern develops because acquiring new information feels easier and more immediately rewarding than the slow, often uncomfortable work of changing established habits and thought patterns. Reading about gratitude practices gives you an instant sense of inspiration and possibility, while actually practicing gratitude daily for months requires consistency and patience that don't provide the same immediate emotional payoff.

The modern self-help industry inadvertently reinforces this consumption approach by constantly promoting new concepts, techniques, and frameworks that promise to be the breakthrough you've been searching for. Publishers and speakers need to differentiate their offerings from everything else available, so they emphasize novelty and revolutionary approaches rather than the deep integration of timeless principles that actually create lasting change.

This creates a marketplace where consumers are encouraged to keep seeking the next great insight rather than fully implementing what they've already learned. You start to believe that your lack of transformation indicates you haven't found the right system yet, rather than recognizing that you haven't fully applied any system long enough to experience its benefits.

The sheer volume of available wisdom also creates decision paralysis that prevents deep engagement with any particular approach. When you have dozens of books recommending different meditation techniques, relationship strategies, and productivity systems, choosing one approach and sticking with it long enough to see results feels limiting rather than focusing. You worry that you might be missing something better, so you keep sampling new approaches without mastering any of them.

This sampling mentality treats wisdom like a buffet where you're supposed to try everything rather than like a practice that requires sustained attention and gradual development. But wisdom integration works more like learning a musical instrument than like trying different foods. You need to commit to one approach long enough to develop real skill before you can effectively incorporate elements from other methods.

Information overload also prevents the deep reflection and contemplation that allow insights to move from intellectual understanding to embodied knowing. When you're constantly consuming new content, your mind stays focused on processing input rather than integrating what you've already received. The space between learning sessions where real integration happens gets filled with more learning, creating a cycle where you know more and more but embody less and less.

The social aspect of wisdom consumption can also become problematic when collecting insights becomes a way to signal intelligence, spiritual development, or personal growth to others rather than a genuine commitment to transformation. You might find yourself sharing quotes on social media, discussing concepts at dinner parties, or recommending books to friends as a way to demonstrate your engagement with personal development rather than as natural overflow from your own applied learning.

This performative aspect of wisdom consumption creates pressure to always be learning something new and impressive rather than deeply integrating basic principles that might not seem sophisticated but create profound changes when consistently applied. Practicing gratitude daily for six months isn't as interesting to talk about as the latest neuroscience research on happiness, but it will transform your life in ways that knowing about neuroscience never will.

The entertainment value of consuming wisdom also becomes addictive because learning new things stimulates the same reward centers in your brain that respond to other forms of novelty and stimulation. Reading about breakthrough techniques or listening to inspiring speakers provides a chemical high that feels like progress even when no actual change occurs in your daily life.

This biochemical reward system makes wisdom consumption feel productive and meaningful even when it's primarily serving as sophisticated procrastination. You get the satisfaction of working on yourself without the vulnerability and uncertainty that come with actually changing how you think, feel, and behave in real-world situations.

The perfectionism that drives many people toward endless learning also prevents implementation because no single approach seems complete or perfect enough to deserve full commitment. You read about meditation and think it would be more effective if combined with journaling. You learn about journaling and decide it needs to include gratitude practice. You discover gratitude techniques and feel they should be enhanced with visualization exercises.

This perfectionist thinking creates elaborate systems that look comprehensive but are too complex to maintain consistently. Instead of starting with simple practices and allowing them to evolve naturally, you design ideal approaches that require more time, energy, and discipline than you actually have available, then abandon them when they prove unsustainable.

The solution isn't to stop learning or to dismiss the value of wisdom from books, teachers, and experiences. The solution is to shift your relationship with learning from consumption to integration, treating each insight as raw material for personal transformation rather than finished products to be collected and stored. This requires developing systems for capturing, processing, and applying wisdom that prioritize depth over breadth and embodiment over information.

The Wisdom Integration Process

True wisdom integration transforms insights from intellectual concepts into lived principles through a systematic process that bridges the gap between knowing and being, turning the accumulated knowledge in your head into automatic responses that guide your decisions and shape your character without requiring conscious effort to maintain. This integration happens through specific practices that move wisdom through stages of understanding, from initial recognition through experimental application to embodied mastery.

The process begins with conscious selection of insights that resonate deeply with your current life situation and growth edges, rather than trying to implement everything you've learned simultaneously. Most people attempt to apply dozens of concepts at once, which dilutes their attention and prevents any of them from taking root deeply enough to create lasting change.

This selection process involves reviewing your accumulated wisdom to identify patterns and themes that appear consistently across different sources and time periods. When multiple books, teachers, and experiences point toward similar principles, that repetition indicates concepts that deserve focused attention. Your intuitive response to different insights also provides guidance about which wisdom is ready to be integrated now versus which might be more relevant for future stages of your development.

The capture phase involves documenting selected insights in ways that preserve their essential meaning while connecting them to your specific circumstances and challenges. Instead of copying quotes or concepts verbatim, you translate wisdom into language that reflects your understanding and relates directly to situations you face regularly. This personalization makes abstract principles concrete and actionable in your daily experience.

Effective capture also includes identifying the underlying principles behind specific techniques or practices rather than just collecting surface-level instructions. For example, instead of noting that you should practice gratitude by writing three things you appreciate each morning, you capture the deeper principle that deliberately focusing on positive aspects of your experience shifts your perceptual habits and emotional baseline in ways that improve your overall life satisfaction and relationship quality.

The experimentation phase involves testing selected insights through small, consistent applications that allow you to experience their effects directly rather than just understanding them intellectually. This experimental approach treats wisdom like hypotheses to be tested in your real-life laboratory rather than truths to be believed based on authority or logic alone. You discover which insights actually work for your personality, circumstances, and goals through direct experience rather than theoretical analysis.

These experiments need to be specific enough to generate clear feedback about effectiveness while being small enough to maintain consistently during busy or stressful periods. Instead of committing to hour-long meditation sessions, you might experiment with three minutes of focused breathing each morning. Instead of trying to transform your entire approach to relationships, you might practice asking just one better question during conversations each day.

The reflection component allows you to process what you're learning from your experiments and adjust your approach based on real-world feedback rather than predetermined expectations about how wisdom should work. This involves regular review of which practices are creating positive changes, which are feeling forced or ineffective, and which need modification to work better with your actual lifestyle and personality.

Weekly reflection sessions provide structured time for this processing, helping you recognize patterns and progress that might not be obvious during daily implementation. You ask yourself questions like "What insights am I actually living this week versus just knowing intellectually?" and "Which practices are becoming more natural versus which still require significant conscious effort?" and "What adjustments would make applying my wisdom more effective or sustainable?"

The integration phase involves gradually expanding successful experiments into broader life patterns while allowing unsuccessful ones to fade away without judgment or self-criticism. Not every insight will work for every person or every life situation, and part of wisdom integration involves learning to distinguish between universal principles and approaches that work better for other people's circumstances or personality types.

This expansion happens naturally as small practices prove their value and begin to influence related areas of your life. A simple gratitude practice might expand into appreciation for challenges and difficulties, not just obvious blessings. A basic meditation routine might evolve into mindful awareness throughout daily activities. A communication technique might become an overall approach to creating deeper connections in all your relationships.

The embodiment stage represents the completion of wisdom integration, when insights have become so natural that they operate automatically without conscious management or effort. At this level, wisdom has transformed from something you do into something you are. You don't practice gratitude; you naturally see life through grateful eyes. You don't use communication techniques; you instinctively create connection through how you interact with people.

This embodiment typically takes months or years of consistent application, but it creates the kind of transformation that feels effortless to maintain because it's become part of your identity rather than behaviors you're trying to sustain through willpower. The wisdom has been integrated so completely that abandoning it would feel unnatural, like trying to speak a different language or use your non-dominant hand for everything.

The process also includes systems for continuing to learn and grow while maintaining focus on deep integration of core principles. Instead of abandoning your established practices every time you encounter new insights, you develop the ability to evaluate new information against your existing foundation and determine whether it enhances what you're already doing or represents a completely different approach that would require starting over.

This mature approach to learning allows you to benefit from new insights without constantly changing directions or abandoning practices that are working well. You become someone who learns continuously while also living consistently from integrated wisdom rather than someone who knows a lot but applies little of what they've learned.

Identifying and Applying Your Core Life Principles

Your core life principles represent the essential truths that guide your decisions and define your character when you're operating from your highest self rather than reacting from conditioning, fear, or social pressure. These principles emerge from distilling years of learning and experience into fundamental guidelines that provide clarity and direction regardless of changing circumstances or external pressures that might otherwise leave you feeling confused or conflicted about how to proceed.

The identification process begins with examining moments in your life when you felt most aligned, proud, and authentic to discover the values and principles you were embodying during those experiences. These peak moments provide clues about who you are when you're not trying to be someone else or meet external expectations, revealing the core principles that create satisfaction and integrity when you honor them consistently.

You might reflect on times when you stood up for something important despite social pressure, made difficult decisions that felt right even when they were costly, or handled challenges in ways that you later recognized as expressions of your best self. What principles were you following during these experiences? What values were you honoring? What beliefs about how life should be lived were you expressing through your actions?

The distillation process involves identifying common themes across different sources of wisdom you've encountered while filtering out concepts that sound good intellectually but don't generate genuine energy or commitment when you consider applying them consistently. Your core principles should feel both inspiring and achievable, challenging you to grow while being realistic about your actual capacity and circumstances.

These principles also need to be personally meaningful rather than universally applicable, reflecting your unique combination of values, experiences, and aspirations rather than generic advice that could apply to anyone. While principles like honesty and kindness might be universally valuable, your specific understanding and application of these concepts should reflect your individual journey and the particular ways you're called to express these values.

Effective core principles are stated positively rather than as restrictions or prohibitions, focusing on who you want to become and how you want to show up rather than what you want to avoid or stop doing. Instead of "Don't be reactive in relationships," a positive principle might be "Respond to others from curiosity and compassion rather than defensiveness." This positive framing creates energy for growth rather than resistance to change.

The application process involves translating abstract principles into specific behavioral guidelines that can inform daily decisions and responses to common situations you encounter regularly. This translation makes your principles practical and actionable rather than inspiring ideas that remain disconnected from how you actually live your life when faced with real choices and challenges.

For example, if one of your core principles is "Live with authentic expression," you might develop specific applications like "Share my real thoughts and feelings in conversations rather than just agreeing to avoid conflict," "Choose work that aligns with my values even if it means less money or status," and "Dress and decorate my space in ways that reflect my personality rather than what others expect."

These specific applications provide concrete guidance for implementing your principles while allowing flexibility in how they're expressed in different contexts and relationships. The same principle of authentic expression might look different in professional settings versus intimate relationships, but the underlying commitment to honesty and genuineness remains consistent.

Regular principle review helps you assess whether you're actually living according to your stated values or just thinking about them occasionally while operating from different priorities in your daily decisions. This review involves honest examination of recent choices and behaviors to identify gaps between your principles and your actions, not for self-criticism but for course correction and renewed commitment.

Weekly principle reflection might involve asking yourself questions like "Which of my core principles did I honor well this week?" and "Where did I act in ways that contradicted my stated values?" and "What situations triggered me to abandon my principles, and how can I prepare differently for similar challenges?" This reflection builds self-awareness while strengthening your commitment to principle-based living.

The integration of principles with decision-making involves developing the habit of consulting your core values before making choices rather than only considering immediate consequences or external pressures. This consultation doesn't need to be elaborate or time-consuming, but it should happen consistently enough that principle-based decision-making becomes automatic rather than something you only remember during major life choices.

This might involve asking yourself simple questions before decisions: "Which choice honors my core principles?" or "What would I do if I were operating from my highest self?" or "How can I handle this situation in ways that reflect who I want to be?" These questions help you access your deeper wisdom rather than just reacting from conditioning or immediate emotions.

Principle-based living also requires developing the courage to act according to your values even when it's inconvenient, unpopular, or costly in the short term. This courage develops gradually as you experience the long-term satisfaction that comes from living with integrity and the internal conflict that results from betraying your own values for temporary advantages or social approval.

The strength to follow your principles consistently comes from recognizing that compromising your core values always creates more problems than it solves, even when honoring them requires difficult conversations, financial sacrifice, or social disapproval. Living according to your principles builds self-respect and authentic confidence that no external achievement can provide.

Your core principles also evolve as you grow and learn, but this evolution happens gradually through deepening understanding rather than frequent changes that prevent any principle from taking root deeply enough to guide your behavior consistently. Mature principle-based living involves commitment to core values while allowing your understanding and application of those values to develop through experience and reflection.

This evolutionary approach prevents both rigid fundamentalism that can't adapt to new circumstances and constant changing that prevents principles from providing stable guidance for your decisions and character development. You remain committed to your deepest values while allowing your expression of those values to become more sophisticated and effective over time.

The Teaching Test: Solidifying Wisdom Through Sharing

Teaching others what you're learning represents the final stage of wisdom integration because it requires you to understand concepts deeply enough to explain them clearly while living them authentically enough that your teaching emerges from embodied experience rather than theoretical knowledge. This teaching process reveals gaps in your understanding and application while strengthening your commitment to the principles you're sharing with others.

The teaching test doesn't require formal educational roles or public speaking opportunities. They can happen through casual conversations, mentoring relationships, parenting interactions, and any situation where you share insights that have proven valuable in your own experience. The key is that your teaching emerges naturally from your growth rather than from a desire to appear knowledgeable or to fix other people's problems.

Authentic teaching happens when people notice positive changes in your life and ask what you've been doing differently, when friends seek your perspective on challenges you've navigated successfully, or when family members want to understand approaches you're using that seem to be working well. This organic teaching feels natural and helpful rather than preachy or superior because it's based on demonstrated results rather than theoretical understanding.

The process of explaining insights to others forces you to clarify your own understanding and identify aspects of wisdom that you thought you had integrated but actually only comprehended intellectually. When someone asks you to explain how you developed more patience or improved your relationships, you quickly discover whether your changes came from deep understanding or superficial technique application.

This clarity test reveals whether you can articulate the underlying principles behind your practices rather than just describing the surface-level actions you've been taking. If you can only tell someone to "practice gratitude" without explaining why it works or how to adapt the practice to their specific circumstances, you probably haven't integrated gratitude deeply enough to teach it effectively.

Teaching also requires you to live more consistently according to the principles you're sharing because people learn more from observing your behavior than from listening to your words. When you know that others are watching how you handle stress, relationships, or challenges, you become more conscious of whether your actions align with the wisdom you're advocating.

This accountability effect strengthens your own practice because inconsistency between your teaching and your living creates internal dissonance that motivates greater alignment. You naturally become more committed to embodying what you teach because you recognize that your credibility and effectiveness depend on authentic demonstration rather than eloquent explanation.

The questions that people ask when you share wisdom also help you deepen your understanding by forcing you to consider applications and perspectives you might not have explored on your own. Someone might ask how your gratitude practice works during grief, how you maintain boundaries without being harsh, or how you trust intuition when making financial decisions. These questions push you to develop a more sophisticated and nuanced understanding.

Effective wisdom sharing also requires learning to meet people where they are, rather than overwhelming them with everything you've learned or expecting them to implement advanced practices before they've mastered basic ones. This skill of appropriate teaching helps you remember your own learning journey and appreciate the gradual process through which wisdom becomes integrated rather than expecting immediate transformation.

The teaching process includes learning to share your failures and struggles alongside your successes because authentic wisdom teaching acknowledges that growth involves setbacks and challenges rather than linear progress toward perfection. When you can discuss how you've recovered from lapses in your practices or learned from mistakes in applying principles, your teaching becomes more relatable and encouraging.

This vulnerability in teaching also prevents the spiritual pride that can develop when you start to see yourself as more advanced or enlightened than others, rather than simply further along in specific areas while still learning and growing in many others. Honest teaching keeps you humble and connected to your ongoing development rather than creating false superiority.

Teaching through modeling represents the most powerful form of wisdom sharing because it demonstrates principles in action rather than just describing them intellectually. When people observe you responding to challenges with patience, treating others with genuine respect, or maintaining joy during difficult periods, they learn more about those qualities than any explanation could provide.

This modeling approach requires you to embody wisdom consistently rather than just understanding it conceptually, which accelerates your own integration while providing authentic examples for others to learn from. Your life becomes a demonstration of the principles you value rather than a contradiction of the wisdom you espouse.

The ripple effects of authentic teaching extend far beyond the immediate people you interact with because wisdom shared from genuine embodiment tends to spread naturally as those people apply what they've learned and share it with others in their circles. This multiplication effect means that your commitment to integrating wisdom deeply can influence many more people than you directly teach.

These ripple effects also create a sense of meaningful contribution that motivates continued learning and growth because you recognize that your personal development serves purposes beyond your individual satisfaction. When your wisdom integration helps others live better lives, your commitment to continued growth feels like service rather than self-improvement.

The teaching test ultimately reveals whether you've moved from collecting insights to living your truth because authentic teaching can only emerge from embodied wisdom rather than accumulated information. When you can share what you've learned in ways that help others while continuing to grow through the teaching process itself, you've achieved the integration that transforms knowledge into wisdom and wisdom into character.

Treasured Wisdom Implementation Process

The endless accumulation of wisdom without application has become sophisticated procrastination that creates the illusion of progress while maintaining familiar patterns that feel safe but don't serve your growth. True wisdom integration requires shifting from consumption to embodiment through systematic processes that move insights from intellectual understanding to lived principles that guide your decisions and shape your character automatically.

The wisdom integration process involves conscious selection of core insights, experimental application through small, consistent practices, regular reflection on what's working, and gradual expansion of successful approaches until they become natural parts of your identity. Your core life principles emerge from distilling accumulated learning into essential truths that provide guidance regardless of changing circumstances, while teaching others what you're learning solidifies your integration and reveals gaps in your understanding.

Your first implementation step is to conduct a wisdom audit of your accumulated learning by reviewing books, notes, and insights you've collected to identify three to five principles that appear consistently across different sources and resonate deeply with your current growth edges. Look for themes and patterns rather than specific techniques, focusing on underlying truths that could guide multiple areas of your life rather than narrow applications.

Write these selected principles in your own words, connecting them specifically to situations you face regularly and challenges you're currently navigating. Instead of copying abstract concepts, translate wisdom into language that reflects your understanding and provides concrete guidance for your actual circumstances and relationships.

Your second step is to choose one core principle and design a simple daily experiment that allows you to test its effectiveness through direct experience rather than theoretical analysis. This experiment should be specific enough to generate clear feedback while being small enough to maintain consistently during busy periods, requiring no more than five to ten minutes of daily attention.

For example, if your selected principle is "respond from curiosity rather than defensiveness," your experiment might involve pausing to ask one genuine question when you feel criticized or challenged, rather than immediately explaining or justifying your position. Track what happens when you apply this approach versus when you react automatically from old patterns.

Your third step is to establish a weekly wisdom review where you reflect on which insights you're actually living versus just knowing intellectually, which practices are becoming more natural versus which still require significant conscious effort, and what adjustments would make your application more effective or sustainable. Use this review to course-correct quickly rather than drifting away from integration gradually.

During this review, honestly assess gaps between your stated principles and your actual behavior without harsh self-criticism, treating inconsistencies as information for improvement rather than evidence of personal failure. Ask yourself what situations trigger you to abandon your principles and how you can prepare differently for similar challenges in the future.

Your fourth step is to identify one person in your life who would benefit from the wisdom you're successfully integrating and look for natural opportunities to share what you're learning through casual conversation, example, or response to their questions rather than unsolicited advice or formal teaching. Focus on sharing from your experience rather than from theoretical knowledge, discussing both successes and struggles in your application process.

This teaching opportunity will reveal whether you understand your chosen principles deeply enough to explain them clearly and live them consistently enough that your sharing feels authentic rather than hypo-critical. Use questions and challenges from others to deepen your own understanding and identify areas where your integration needs further development.

Your final step is to create a simple note-taking system for capturing new insights without abandoning your focus on integrating core principles you've already selected. When you encounter compelling new wisdom through books, conversations, or experiences, note it briefly but resist the temptation to immediately start experimenting with new approaches before your current practices have become natural.

This system might involve keeping a separate list of "future integration" insights that you review quarterly to determine whether they enhance your existing principles or represent entirely different approaches that would require starting over. This prevents the constant direction changes that keep you perpetually learning but never deeply embodying any particular wisdom.

Track your wisdom integration using the daily question **"Did I capture or apply wisdom today?"** focusing on both learning from your experiences and implementing insights you've already gathered. The goal is to become someone who learns continuously while living consistently from integrated principles.

8

S is for SELF-LOVE and CARE

You know that voice in your head, the one that never seems to take a break from pointing out everything you're doing wrong, everything you should be doing better, and all the ways you don't measure up to some impossible standard you can't even clearly define. It's the voice that tells you you're being lazy when you need rest, selfish when you consider your own needs, and weak when you struggle with challenges that would overwhelm anyone.

This internal critic has convinced you that harsh self-judgment motivates positive change, that being hard on yourself prevents complacency and mediocrity. You've learned to treat yourself worse than you would treat a stranger, speaking to yourself in ways you would never speak to someone you care about, setting expectations that you would never impose on others.

The cruel irony is that this self-criticism actually prevents the very changes you're trying to create. When you constantly berate yourself for mistakes, judge yourself for having needs, and demand perfection in areas where you're still learning, you create internal conditions that make growth more difficult rather than easier. Your nervous system interprets self-attack as danger, triggering stress responses that cloud your thinking and drain your energy for positive action.

Self-compassion isn't weakness or self-indulgence; it's the foundation that makes sustainable transformation possible. When you treat yourself with the same kindness you would show a beloved friend, you create emotional safety that allows authentic growth to flourish. This chapter will show you how to transform your relationship with yourself from your harshest critic to your most supportive ally.

Self-Criticism Keeps You Stuck

Your inner critic developed as a well-intentioned but misguided attempt to protect you from rejection, failure, and disappointment by identifying potential problems before others could point them out and motivating you to meet standards that would ensure acceptance and success. This internal voice learned to scan constantly for flaws, mistakes, and inadequacies, believing that catching these issues early would help you fix them before they caused real consequences in your relationships or achievements.

The critical voice also absorbed messages from authority figures who used shame and criticism as motivational tools, teachers who focused on mistakes rather than progress, parents who expressed love conditionally based on performance, and cultural messages that equated self-worth with productivity and achievement. These external critics became internalized, creating a mental environment where you learned to evaluate yourself through harsh judgment rather than compassionate assessment.

This self-critical approach might have provided some protection during childhood when you were dependent on others for survival and needed to adapt quickly to expectations and demands. The ability to anticipate criticism and adjust behavior accordingly could prevent punishment, rejection, or abandonment in environments where love and acceptance were conditional on meeting certain standards or avoiding particular mistakes.

But what served as a survival strategy in childhood becomes self-sabotage in adulthood because the conditions that made harsh self-judgment necessary no longer exist. You're no longer dependent on others for basic survival, and the relationships and opportunities available to you now can actually be damaged by the perfectionism and self-attack that might have provided protection in less secure environments.

The self-criticism trap operates by convincing you that without constant internal pressure and judgment, you would become lazy, careless, and mediocre. Your inner critic argues that relaxing standards or treating yourself with kindness would lead to complacency and poor performance, that you need harsh motivation to maintain discipline and achieve your goals. This belief keeps you trapped in cycles of self-attack even when you can see that the criticism isn't creating the positive changes it promises.

Research reveals the opposite of what your inner critic claims: self-compassion actually increases motivation, resilience, and performance by creating internal conditions where learning and growth can occur naturally. When you treat mistakes as information rather than evidence of inadequacy, you recover more quickly from setbacks and apply lessons more effectively. When you acknowledge your efforts alongside your results, you maintain energy for continued improvement rather than burning out from constant self-judgment.

The trap also operates through perfectionism that sets impossible standards and then criticizes you for failing to meet them. Your inner critic demands that you handle every situation flawlessly, never make mistakes, always know what to do, and consistently perform at peak levels regardless of circumstances, energy levels, or competing demands on your attention. These unrealistic expectations guarantee failure and provide constant fuel for self-criticism.

This perfectionist thinking ignores the reality that growth involves making mistakes, learning requires experimenting with approaches that don't always work, and mastery develops gradually through practice rather than appearing fully formed from the beginning. When you demand perfection from yourself, you're essentially criticizing yourself for being human and following the same learning processes that everyone must navigate to develop new skills and capacities.

Self-criticism also creates a vicious cycle where the stress and emotional depletion caused by internal attack makes you more likely to make the very mistakes and poor choices that your inner critic then uses as evidence for more criticism. When you're constantly under internal assault, your nervous system operates in survival mode, which impairs decision-making, creativity, and emotional regulation. Exactly the capacities you need to perform well and make good choices.

The energy drain caused by constant self-judgment also leaves you with fewer resources for the positive actions and changes you're trying to create. Instead of directing your mental and emotional energy toward growth and improvement, you waste enormous amounts of energy on internal battles that don't produce any constructive outcomes. You become exhausted from fighting yourself rather than energized by working toward meaningful goals.

The trap becomes particularly insidious when self-criticism masquerades as self-awareness or personal responsibility. You might believe that acknowledging your flaws and mistakes harshly demonstrates maturity and accountability, when actually it often represents avoidance of the more challenging work of understanding why problems occurred and what specific actions would create better outcomes. Self-attack feels like you're doing something about problems when you're actually just creating additional problems.

Breaking free from the self-criticism trap requires recognizing that your inner critic's promises are false. Harsh self-judgment doesn't create lasting motivation, prevent future mistakes, or improve your performance. Instead, it creates internal conditions that make positive change more difficult while consuming energy that could be directed toward actual improvement and growth.

The alternative isn't lowering your standards or becoming complacent about areas where you want to grow. The alternative is treating yourself with the same combination of honesty and kindness that you would offer to someone you love who was facing similar challenges. This compassionate approach provides accurate assessment of situations while creating emotional safety that supports learning, risk-taking, and sustained effort toward meaningful goals.

Rewriting Your Internal Dialogue

The conversation you have with yourself throughout each day shapes your emotional state, energy levels, and capacity for positive action more than any external circumstance or relationship dynamic. Most people are completely unconscious of this internal dialogue, allowing automatic patterns of self-talk to run unchecked even when those patterns create stress, discouragement, and self-sabotage that undermines their efforts to create positive changes in their lives.

Becoming aware of your internal dialogue requires developing the observer part of your mind that can notice thoughts without being completely identified with them, creating enough psychological distance to recognize patterns in your self-talk and choose more supportive alternatives when automatic responses aren't serving your wellbeing or growth. This observer capacity develops through practice and allows you to become the author of your internal experience rather than the victim of unconscious mental habits.

Self-love is not just what you do for yourself; it's the attitude you hold toward yourself while you're doing it.

You can follow every exercise in this book and still stay stuck if your inner posture is harsh, impatient, or ashamed. When I used to tell my children, "Attitude is so important," I wasn't only talking about their attitude toward life, but also their attitude toward themselves when they struggled. The same is true here: the more kindness, curiosity, and respect you bring to your own growth, the more the G.I.F.T.S. practices can actually take root.

The first step in rewriting internal dialogue involves catching self-critical thoughts in real time rather than only noticing them during reflection or when they've already created emotional damage. This real-time awareness develops gradually as you learn to recognize the physical and emotional signals that accompany harsh self-judgment, the tightening in your chest, the sinking feeling in your stomach, or the sudden drain of energy that occurs when your inner critic launches an attack.

These body signals often provide earlier warning than conscious recognition of critical thoughts because your nervous system responds to internal attack before your rational mind processes what's happening. Learning to notice these physical cues allows you to interrupt self-critical patterns before they gain momentum and create the emotional spiral that makes supportive self-talk feel impossible or artificial.

Once you catch self-critical thoughts, the rewriting process involves asking yourself how you would speak to a beloved friend who was facing the same situation or challenge that triggered your self-attack. This question bypasses your habitual self-judgment patterns and accesses the natural compassion and wisdom you already possess but rarely direct toward yourself. Most people are much kinder and more encouraging to others than they are to themselves.

The friend test reveals the double standard you apply to yourself versus others and provides immediate access to more supportive language that maintains honesty about challenges while offering encouragement and perspective that actually helps rather than harms. Instead of "You're so stupid for making that mistake," you might say, "That was a difficult situation, and you did your best with the information you had. What can you learn from this experience?"

Effective internal dialogue rewriting also involves distinguishing between self-compassion and self-pity, between honest assessment and harsh judgment, and between accountability and attack. Self-compassion acknowledges difficulties and mistakes while maintaining belief in your capacity to learn and grow. Self-pity wallows in problems without taking constructive action. Honest assessment identifies what happened and why without character assassination. Harsh judgment makes global conclusions about your worth based on specific incidents.

The language you use in internal dialogue matters enormously because words carry emotional energy that either supports or undermines your capacity for positive action. Words like "always" and "never" create hopelessness by suggesting that patterns are permanent and unchangeable. Words like "should" and "must" create pressure and resistance by implying that your natural responses are wrong or inadequate. Words like "failure" and "disaster" catastrophize normal learning experiences.

Replacing inflammatory language with neutral or supportive alternatives changes the emotional impact of your internal dialogue without denying reality or avoiding responsibility. Instead of "I always mess up relationships," you might think "I'm learning how to create healthy relationships and sometimes I make mistakes in that process." Instead of "I should be further along by now," you might think "I'm making progress at my own pace and that's okay."

The rewriting process also includes developing specific supportive phrases that you can use consistently when facing common challenges or setbacks that typically trigger self-criticism. Having prepared responses prevents you from having to generate compassionate self-talk in moments when you're already stressed or discouraged and your inner critic is most active and persuasive.

These prepared phrases might include "I'm learning and growing, and mistakes are part of that process," "I'm doing my best with the resources and understanding I have right now," "This is difficult, and it's okay that I'm struggling," "I can handle this challenge one step at a time," and "I deserve the same kindness I would show to anyone else facing this situation."

The supportive internal dialogue also needs to include celebration and acknowledgment of efforts, progress, and positive qualities rather than only addressing problems and mistakes. Most people's internal dialogue focuses disproportionately on what's wrong while ignoring what's going well, creating a distorted perspective that undermines confidence and motivation. Balanced internal dialogue includes appreciation for what you're doing well alongside honest assessment of areas for improvement.

This appreciative aspect of internal dialogue might involve noticing when you handle situations better than you would have in the past, acknowledging efforts you're making even when results aren't perfect yet, and recognizing positive qualities you demonstrate in your relationships and responsibilities. This isn't false praise or denial of genuine challenges, but rather accurate recognition of the full picture of your experience and development.

The rewriting process requires patience and persistence because automatic self-talk patterns have been strengthened through years of repetition and won't change overnight through conscious effort alone. The goal is gradual improvement in the tone and content of your internal dialogue rather than perfect self-compassion that never lapses into old critical patterns. Each time you catch and redirect self-critical thoughts, you're building new neural pathways that make supportive self-talk more automatic over time.

Consistency matters more than perfection in developing new internal dialogue patterns. It's better to make small improvements in how you speak to yourself daily than to have occasional periods of perfect self-compassion followed by extended returns to harsh self-judgment. The cumulative effect of slightly kinder internal dialogue creates significant changes in your emotional baseline and capacity for sustained positive action.

Self-Care That Restores You

Most approaches to self-care focus on surface-level activities that provide temporary pleasure or relaxation without addressing the deeper needs for restoration, meaning, and authentic nourishment that actually sustain your capacity to show up fully for your responsibilities and relationships. True self-care involves understanding what genuinely restores your energy, clarity, and emotional equilibrium rather than just what feels good in the moment or looks like proper self-care from the outside.

The commercialized version of self-care promotes consumption-based solutions like spa treatments, shopping, expensive vacations, or luxury products that promise to make you feel better but often leave you feeling empty or guilty afterward because they don't address the underlying depletion or provide lasting restoration. While these activities might offer temporary relief, they don't build the internal resources and life conditions that prevent burnout and create sustainable wellbeing.

Authentic self-care begins with an honest assessment of what actually drains your energy versus what restores it, recognizing that these patterns are individual and might not match what works for other people or what popular culture suggests should be nourishing. Some people find social interaction energizing, while others need solitude to recharge. Some people restore through physical activity, while others need complete rest. Some people feel nourished by creative expression, while others prefer structured learning or problem-solving.

This personalized approach requires paying attention to how you feel before and after different activities, relationships, and environments, rather than assuming that certain experiences should be restorative based on their reputation or other people's recommendations. You might discover that activities you thought were relaxing actually create subtle stress, or that responsibilities you considered draining actually provide energy when approached with the right mindset.

Physical self-care involves meeting your body's basic needs for nutrition, movement, rest, and medical attention in ways that support your overall energy and health rather than just following generic recommendations that might not match your individual constitution and circumstances. This means learning to distinguish between what your body actually needs versus what you think you should want or what would be most convenient or socially acceptable.

Your body provides constant feedback about what supports its optimal functioning through energy levels, sleep quality, mood stability, and physical comfort, but most people have learned to override these signals in favor of external schedules and expectations. Authentic physical self-care involves rebuilding sensitivity to your body's wisdom while creating life structures that allow you to honor what you discover about your genuine needs.

This might mean eating foods that actually make you feel energized rather than foods you think are healthy, moving your body in ways that feel good rather than exercise routines you believe you should follow, and sleeping according to your natural rhythms when possible rather than forcing yourself into schedules that leave you chronically tired. The goal is working with your body's natural tendencies rather than constantly fighting against them.

Emotional self-care involves creating internal and external conditions that support your psychological wellbeing and capacity for emotional regulation rather than just managing stress after it accumulates. This includes setting boundaries that protect your energy from excessive demands, spending time with people who appreciate and support you, and engaging in activities that generate genuine joy and satisfaction rather than just distraction from problems.

Effective emotional self-care also involves developing skills for processing difficult emotions rather than just avoiding them or numbing them through various forms of escapism. This means learning to sit with sadness, anger, fear, and disappointment without immediately trying to fix or change these feelings, allowing them to move through your system naturally rather than getting stuck as chronic emotional tension.

Mental self-care includes protecting your mind from excessive stimulation and negativity while providing it with input that supports clear thinking and emotional stability. This involves conscious choices about what media you consume, what conversations you engage in, and how much information you try to process simultaneously. Your mental environment affects your mood and energy as much as your physical environment.

This mental hygiene might involve limiting news consumption that creates anxiety without providing actionable information, avoiding social media that triggers comparison and inadequacy, and choosing entertainment that leaves you feeling inspired or peaceful rather than agitated or depleted. You might also need to set boundaries with people who consistently drain your energy through complaining, drama, or criticism.

Spiritual self-care addresses your need for meaning, connection to something larger than yourself, and alignment with your deeper values and purposes. This doesn't necessarily involve religious practices but includes any activities that help you feel connected to what matters most to you and remind you of your place in the larger web of life and relationships.

This spiritual dimension might involve time in nature, creative expression, service to others, meditation or prayer, reading wisdom literature, or simply regular reflection on what you're grateful for and what gives your life meaning. The specific practices matter less than the sense of connection and purpose they provide.

Restorative self-care also includes saying no to requests and opportunities that don't align with your current capacity or priorities, even when those opportunities seem valuable or when declining might disappoint others. Learning to protect your time and energy for what matters most to you requires developing comfort with others' disappointment and your own fear of missing out on potentially beneficial experiences.

This selective approach to commitments allows you to show up fully for the responsibilities and relationships you do choose rather than spreading yourself so thin that you can't be present or effective anywhere. Quality of engagement matters more than quantity of activities when it comes to creating a fulfilling and sustainable life.

The goal of authentic self-care is creating conditions where you naturally feel energized, clear, and emotionally stable, rather than constantly recovering from depletion or managing stress that could have been prevented through better boundaries and life design. When self-care becomes integrated into your daily routine rather than something you do occasionally when you're already burned out, it supports sustained capacity for contributing to others and pursuing meaningful goals.

Self-Compassion

Self-compassion represents a fundamental shift in how you relate to your own suffering, mistakes, and imperfections, treating yourself with the same kindness and understanding you would naturally offer to a beloved friend facing similar challenges. This practice doesn't eliminate difficulties from your life but transforms how you experience and respond to inevitable human struggles in ways that support healing and growth rather than creating additional suffering through self-attack and isolation.

The foundation of self-compassion involves recognizing that suffering, imperfection, and failure are universal human experiences rather than personal inadequacies that separate you from others or indicate something fundamentally wrong with you. When you make mistakes, face rejection, or struggle with challenges, you're participating in the common human experience rather than revealing unique flaws that make you unworthy of love and acceptance.

This recognition of shared humanity helps counteract the isolation and shame that typically accompany difficult experiences, reminding you that everyone faces similar challenges and that your struggles don't make you different or defective compared to others who seem to have their lives more together. Most people are dealing with their own versions of the same basic human challenges around relationships, work, health, and personal growth.

The practice begins with mindful awareness of when you're suffering rather than immediately trying to fix, avoid, or judge your emotional experience. This means noticing when you're feeling sad, anxious, frustrated, or disappointed without automatically launching into problem-solving mode or self-criticism about having these feelings. Simply acknowledging "this is a moment of suffering" or "this is really difficult right now" creates space for compassion to emerge.

This mindful acknowledgment prevents the secondary suffering that comes from judging yourself for having normal human emotions or trying to force yourself to feel differently than you actually do. The original pain of disappointment, loss, or failure is inevitable, but the additional pain of self-criticism and resistance to your experience is optional and often more damaging than the original difficulty.

The core self-compassion practice involves speaking to yourself during difficult moments the way you would speak to someone you love who was going through the same experience. This means using a tone of voice that conveys warmth and understanding rather than criticism and impatience, offering words of encouragement and perspective rather than harsh judgment and catastrophic predictions about the future.

You might place your hand on your heart and say something like "This is really hard right now, and it's okay that I'm struggling. Everyone goes through difficult times like this. I'm not alone, and I don't have to handle this perfectly. I'm doing the best I can with a challenging situation." This physical gesture of placing your hand on your heart activates the parasympathetic nervous system and creates a sense of comfort and safety.

The practice also includes offering yourself the same practical support you would give to a friend in distress. Instead of just criticizing yourself for making a mistake, you might ask, "What do I need right now?" and then provide whatever support would actually be helpful: rest, comfort, problem-solving assistance, or simply patient presence while you process difficult emotions.

This supportive approach might involve making yourself a cup of tea, taking a warm bath, calling a trusted friend, going for a gentle walk, or simply allowing yourself to feel sad without trying to cheer up immediately. The goal is responding to your own distress with the same care and practical help you would naturally offer to someone else you care about.

Self-compassion during mistakes and failures involves distinguishing between your actions and your identity, recognizing that making poor choices or falling short of your goals doesn't make you a bad person but simply means you're human and still learning. This distinction allows you to take responsibility for problems you've created while maintaining self-respect and motivation for making positive changes.

Instead of global self-condemnation like "I'm such an idiot" or "I always mess everything up," self-compassionate responses might include "I made a mistake and I can learn from this experience," "I'm disappointed in my choice but I still believe in my capacity to do better," or "This didn't work out the way I hoped, and that's painful, but it doesn't define my worth as a person."

The practice extends to self-forgiveness for past mistakes and regrets that you can't change but continue to punish yourself for through ongoing self-criticism and shame. Self-forgiveness doesn't excuse harmful behavior or eliminate the need to make amends when possible, but it releases you from the prison of perpetual self-punishment that prevents healing and positive change.

This forgiveness process might involve writing yourself a letter from the perspective of someone who loves you unconditionally, acknowledging the pain you've caused while also recognizing your humanity and capacity for growth. You might also engage in ritual activities that symbolize releasing past mistakes, such as burning written regrets or planting something beautiful in honor of your commitment to doing better in the future.

Daily self-compassion practice involves checking in with yourself regularly throughout the day to notice when you're being self-critical and consciously choosing more supportive internal dialogue. This doesn't require elaborate rituals but simply involves treating yourself with baseline kindness and respect rather than allowing automatic harsh judgment to dominate your internal experience.

The transformative power of self-compassion emerges gradually as you experience the relief of not constantly fighting with yourself and discover that kindness actually motivates positive change more effectively than criticism. When you feel safe and supported internally, you're more willing to take risks, try new approaches, and persist through challenges because you know you'll treat yourself with understanding rather than attack if things don't work out perfectly.

This internal safety also improves your relationships with others because you're not seeking external validation to compensate for internal self-attack, and you're not projecting your self-criticism onto others through judgment and criticism of their imperfections. When you treat yourself with compassion, you naturally extend that same understanding and kindness to the people around you.

Self-Love and Care Implementation Process

The self-criticism trap operates by convincing you that harsh internal judgment motivates positive change when it actually creates conditions that make growth more difficult while consuming energy that could be directed toward actual improvement. Self-compassion provides the emotional safety and internal support that allows authentic transformation to occur naturally, treating yourself with the same kindness you would show a beloved friend while maintaining an honest assessment of areas where you want to grow.

Rewriting your internal dialogue involves catching self-critical thoughts in real time and consciously choosing more supportive language that maintains accountability without character assassination. Authentic self-care addresses your deeper needs for restoration and nourishment rather than just providing temporary pleasure or following generic recommendations that might not match your individual constitution and circumstances.

Your first implementation step is to develop awareness of your internal dialogue by noticing the physical and emotional signals that accompany self-critical thoughts: the tightening in your chest, sinking feeling in your stomach, or sudden energy drain that occurs when your inner critic attacks. Practice catching these signals in real time rather than only noticing them during reflection after emotional damage has already occurred.

When you catch self-critical thoughts, immediately ask yourself "How would I speak to a beloved friend facing this same situation?" and then offer yourself that same tone of kindness and understanding. Replace inflammatory language like "always," "never," "should," and "failure" with neutral or supportive alternatives that acknowledge challenges without creating hopelessness or shame.

Your second step is to create a personalized self-care assessment by paying attention to how you feel before and after different activities, relationships, and environments to discover what actually restores your energy versus what just feels good temporarily or looks like proper self-care from the outside. Notice whether social interaction energizes or drains you, whether you restore through movement or rest, whether you need creative expression or structured learning to feel nourished.

Design your self-care practices around what genuinely supports your physical, emotional, mental, and spiritual wellbeing rather than following generic recommendations or cultural expectations about what should be restorative. This might mean eating foods that make you feel energized, moving in ways that feel good, sleeping according to your natural rhythms, and protecting your mental environment from excessive stimulation and negativity.

Your third step is to establish a daily self-compassion practice by placing your hand on your heart whenever you notice you're suffering and speaking to yourself with the same warmth and understanding you would offer someone you love. Use phrases like "This is really difficult right now and it's okay that I'm struggling," "Everyone goes through challenges like this," and "I'm doing the best I can with a difficult situation."

Practice distinguishing between your actions and your identity when you make mistakes, recognizing that poor choices don't make you a bad person but simply mean you're human and still learning. Instead of global self-condemnation, offer responses like "I made a mistake and I can learn from this" or "I'm disappointed but I still believe in my capacity to do better."

Your fourth step is to develop prepared supportive phrases that you can use consistently when facing common challenges that typically trigger self-criticism. Write down statements like "I'm learning and growing, and mistakes are part of that process," "I deserve the same kindness I would show anyone else," and "I can handle this challenge one step at a time," and practice using them when your inner critic becomes active.

Include appreciation for your efforts, progress, and positive qualities in your internal dialogue rather than only addressing problems and mistakes. Notice when you handle situations better than you would have in the past, acknowledge efforts you're making even when results aren't perfect, and recognize positive qualities you demonstrate in your relationships and responsibilities.

Your final step is to practice self-forgiveness for past mistakes and regrets by writing yourself a letter from the perspective of someone who loves you unconditionally, acknowledging pain you may have caused while recognizing your humanity and capacity for growth. Release yourself from perpetual self-punishment that prevents healing and positive change while maintaining appropriate accountability for making amends when possible.

Track your self-compassion development using the daily question **"Did I do something that demonstrated care for myself today?"** focusing on both internal kindness through supportive self-talk and external care through meeting your genuine needs for restoration and nourishment. The goal is creating internal conditions where you feel safe and supported enough to take risks, try new approaches, and persist through challenges because you know you'll treat yourself with understanding rather than attack, regardless of outcomes.

When self-love and care become integrated into your identity rather than practices you try to maintain, they create the foundation that supports all other areas of the G.I.F.T.S. method while making sustainable contributions possible from a place of fullness rather than depletion.

9

30-DAY G.I.F.T.S. INTEGRATION SYSTEM

Making it Automatic

The moment has arrived to transform everything you've learned into lived reality. The 30-Day G.I.F.T.S. Integration System bridges from understanding to embodiment, from knowing what would improve your life to actually living that way consistently. This isn't another program you'll start with enthusiasm and abandon when motivation fades. It's a systematic approach designed around your real life, with built-in supports that make follow-through inevitable rather than hopeful.

You've spent the previous chapters understanding why traditional approaches to personal development fail and learning the specific practices that create lasting transformation. Now comes the crucial part: implementing everything simultaneously in a way that feels natural rather than overwhelming, sustainable rather than perfect, and integrated rather than fragmented across separate improvement projects.

The system operates on the principle that 30 days provides the perfect timeline for establishing new neural pathways without overwhelming your system, creating momentum while remaining achievable within your busy

124

life. You're not trying to become a completely different person in one month. You're building the foundation for automatic responses that will continue developing long after the initial period ends.

This systematic approach addresses every obstacle that has derailed your previous attempts at change through specific protocols for maintaining consistency, recovering from lapses, handling resistance, and adapting to changing circumstances. By the end of these 30 days, the G.I.F.T.S. practices won't feel like things you're trying to remember to do; they'll feel like natural expressions of who you're becoming.

Why 30 Days for Real Change

Neuroscience research reveals that 30 days provides the optimal window for establishing new neural pathways while avoiding the overwhelm that causes most people to abandon change efforts before they gain momentum. Your brain needs approximately three to four weeks of consistent repetition to begin automating new behaviors, but it also needs to experience success within a timeframe that feels manageable rather than endless or intimidating.

Shorter timeframes like seven or fourteen days don't provide enough repetition for new patterns to feel natural, leaving you dependent on willpower and conscious effort that inevitably get depleted by other life demands. Longer commitments like 90 days or six months feel overwhelming before you start, making it easy to procrastinate beginning or to give up entirely when you encounter the inevitable challenges that arise during any change process.

The 30-day timeline also aligns with natural monthly rhythms that your body and mind recognize as complete cycles, providing psychological satisfaction when you reach the end while creating natural momentum to continue with practices that have proven their value through consistent application. Most people report that beneficial practices feel automatic rather than effortful by day 21 to 25, giving you several days to experience the ease that motivates long-term continuation.

This timeline works particularly well for the integrated G.I.F.T.S. approach because it allows each area to support and strengthen the others rather than competing for your limited attention and energy. Week one establishes basic practices in all five key areas, week two deepens your consistency and begins revealing interconnections, week three integrates the practices into your identity, and week four demonstrates the compound benefits that make continued application feel obvious rather than disciplined.

The 30-day structure also provides enough time to encounter and work through the resistance that emerges when real change starts happening. Your old identity will push back against new patterns somewhere between day 10 and day 20, creating internal conflict, increased stress, or relationship challenges that test your commitment to transformation. Having a clear endpoint helps you persist through these temporary difficulties rather than interpreting them as signs that the approach isn't working.

Research on habit formation shows that consistency matters more than perfection during the initial establishment period, and 30 days provides enough opportunities to recover from missed days without losing momentum entirely. If you maintain your practices 80% of the time during this period, you'll experience significant benefits and establish patterns that continue developing naturally rather than requiring constant conscious management.

The timeline also creates social accountability opportunities that support follow-through without depending on other people's availability or commitment levels. You can share your 30-day commitment with family and friends who will naturally check in on your progress, or you can find others who want to do this simultaneously and create mutual support without formal accountability partnerships that might become burdensome.

Thirty days is long enough to experience real benefits in all five G.I.F.T.S. key areas: improved mood and perspective from gratitude practice, clearer decision-making from intuitive development, deeper relationships from presence and connection practices, applying practical wisdom that improves daily life, and increased energy and self-respect from authentic self-care. These tangible improvements provide motivation that extends far beyond this initial implementation period.

The timeline prevents the perfectionism that sabotages many change efforts because 30 days feels experimental rather than permanent. You're not committing to maintain elaborate practices forever. You're testing an integrated approach for one month to see how it affects your life experience. This experimental mindset reduces pressure and allows you to approach this with curiosity rather than performance anxiety.

Most importantly, 30 days provides enough time for the practices to begin feeling like natural expressions of your personality rather than behaviors you're forcing yourself to maintain. When gratitude, intuitive decision-making, relationship presence, applied wisdom, and self-compassion start feeling automatic, continuing them requires no additional willpower or motivation because they've become integrated into your identity rather than imposed from outside.

The system structure also includes specific protocols for what happens after the initial 30 days, preventing the common problem of reaching your goal and then abandoning the practices that got you there. You'll have clear guidance for maintaining what's working, adjusting what needs modification, and continuing to develop in areas where you want deeper growth without starting over from the beginning.

Your Week-by-Week Implementation Strategy

The weekly progression strategy ensures that you build sustainable practices gradually rather than trying to implement everything perfectly from day one, which typically leads to overwhelm and abandonment within the first week. Each week introduces new elements while reinforcing what you've already established, creating layers of integration that support each other rather than competing for your limited attention and energy.

WEEK ONE

Week one focuses on establishing the basic daily practices in all five G.I.F.T.S. key areas using the simplest possible versions that require minimal time and energy while still creating meaningful contact with each area.

Your gratitude practice involves appreciating three things during existing transition moments throughout your day. Your intuitive intention practice includes pausing before one decision daily to check in with your gut feeling. Your family and friends connection involves one meaningful interaction per day, whether through presence, appreciation, or genuine curiosity about someone's experience.

Applying your treasured wisdom during week one involves capturing one insight daily from any source: books, conversations, experiences, or reflections, and identifying one specific way you could apply that insight within the next 24 hours. Your self-love and care practice includes one daily act that demonstrates kindness toward yourself, whether through supportive internal dialogue, meeting a genuine need, or treating yourself with the same consideration you would show a good friend.

These week one practices are designed to be completed in less than ten minutes total throughout your entire day, integrated into activities you're already doing rather than requiring separate time blocks that compete with existing obligations. The goal is consistency rather than intensity, establishing the habit of daily contact with all five key areas before expanding the depth or duration of any particular practice.

WEEK TWO

Week two deepens your engagement with each area while maintaining the same basic structure, allowing you to experience how the practices begin supporting and reinforcing each other. Your gratitude practice expands to include appreciation for challenges and difficulties alongside obvious blessings, developing the capacity to find meaning and growth opportunities in all your experiences rather than only feeling grateful when things go well.

Your intuitive intention practice during week two includes checking in with your inner guidance before making three decisions daily, ranging from small choices like what to eat or which route to take to medium-sized decisions about how to spend your evening or weekend time. You begin noticing patterns in when your intuition feels clearest and most reliable, building confidence in your ability to access and trust inner wisdom.

Your family and friends connection deepens during week two through practicing presence during conversations, eliminating distractions, and bringing complete attention to the person you're talking with rather than multitasking or preparing your response while they're speaking. You also begin expressing specific appreciation for people's qualities and contributions rather than generic compliments, creating deeper emotional safety and intimacy in your relationships.

Week two wisdom involves reviewing insights you captured during week one to identify which ones you actually implemented versus which remained intellectual concepts, then focusing on deeper integration of the most valuable and practical principles rather than continuing to collect new information. You also begin connecting insights from different sources to identify patterns and themes that deserve sustained attention.

Self-love and care during week two includes developing awareness of your internal dialogue and consciously choosing more supportive language when you catch yourself being self-critical. You also begin identifying what genuinely restores your energy versus what just provides temporary distraction or pleasure, personalizing your self-care practices around your actual needs rather than generic recommendations.

WEEK THREE

Week three represents the integration phase, where individual practices begin connecting naturally without conscious effort to link them together. Your gratitude practice starts including appreciation for your intuitive guidance, your relationships, the wisdom you're gaining, and your own growth and healing. Your decision-making automatically includes consideration of how choices will affect the people you love and whether they align with principles you're developing.

During week three, your relationship interactions naturally include gratitude for the people in your life, intuitive attention to what each relationship needs, application of communication insights you've learned, and self-care boundaries that allow you to show up sustainably rather than giving until you're depleted. These connections happen organically rather than through conscious effort to integrate the areas.

Your wisdom application during week three becomes more sophisticated as you begin distinguishing between insights that deserve immediate implementation, those that need more reflection and preparation, and those that might be valuable for future development but aren't relevant to your current circumstances. You also start recognizing how different principles work together rather than treating them as separate techniques.

Week three self-compassion includes extending kindness to your imperfect implementation of the system itself, treating missed practices as information rather than failures, and recovering quickly from lapses rather than using them as excuses to abandon the entire effort. You begin experiencing the emotional stability that comes from treating yourself as an ally rather than an adversary.

WEEK FOUR

Week four demonstrates the compound benefits that emerge when all five key areas are working together consistently, creating upward spirals where progress in one area automatically supports progress in others. Your gratitude practice enhances your capacity for clear intuitive guidance, which leads to better relationship decisions, which creates emotional safety for applying wisdom and treating yourself with care, which supports deeper gratitude for your life experience.

During the final week, you also begin planning how to maintain and develop what you've established beyond the 30-day implementation period, identifying which practices feel most natural and beneficial while recognizing areas where you want continued growth and development. This planning prevents the common problem of reaching your goal and then gradually abandoning the practices that created the positive changes you're experiencing.

The Daily Check-In

The daily check-in system transforms vague intentions into concrete accountability through a simple five-minute practice that tracks your progress, celebrates small wins, and provides immediate course correction when you drift away from your practices. This system operates independently of other people's availability or commitment levels while creating the consistent feedback loop that turns good intentions into automatic behaviors.

The check-in happens at the same time each day, preferably in the evening when you can review the entire day's experience and plan adjustments for tomorrow. Consistency of timing matters more than the specific time you choose because regular scheduling makes the review automatic rather than something you have to remember to do when you're already tired or distracted by other end-of-day activities.

The system uses five simple yes-or-no questions that correspond to each area of the G.I.F.T.S. method, eliminating the subjective judgment that often leads to discouragement when practices don't feel perfect or transformative.

1. **Did you practice gratitude today?**
2. **Did you check in with your intuition before at least one decision?**
3. **Did you have a meaningful connection with someone you care about?**
4. **Did you capture or apply wisdom?**
5. **Did you do something that demonstrated care for yourself?**

These questions focus on completion rather than quality, giving you credit for any engagement with each area, regardless of how inspired, successful, or profound the experience felt. On days when your gratitude practice feels forced, you still get credit for doing it. When your intuitive guidance seems unclear, you still get credit for pausing to ask. This approach builds consistency rather than perfection, creating the foundation for deeper development over time.

The tracking component involves marking your yes-or-no responses on a simple calendar or chart that provides visual feedback about your patterns over time. Most people are surprised to discover that they're more consistent than their subjective impressions suggest, and seeing several days or weeks of mostly positive responses provides motivation that subjective assessment often lacks because memory tends to focus on lapses rather than successes.

The visual tracking also reveals patterns in when you're most likely to maintain practices versus when you tend to skip them, providing valuable information for optimizing your approach. You might discover that you're consistent during normal weeks but abandon practices entirely when traveling, or that you maintain morning practices well but struggle with evening ones, or that certain life circumstances predictably derail your efforts.

CELEBRATE

The celebration component ensures that you acknowledge progress and positive patterns rather than only noticing when you've missed practices or feel like you're not doing enough. Each day that you answer yes to three or more questions deserves recognition as a successful day, regardless of what else happened or how challenging your circumstances were. This positive reinforcement builds momentum and motivation for continued effort.

Weekly celebration involves reviewing your tracking chart to notice improvements, consistency patterns, and areas where you're developing naturally without forced effort. You might celebrate maintaining practices during a stressful week, or notice that your relationship connections are becoming more natural, or recognize that you're applying wisdom more automatically without having to think about it consciously.

RECOVERY PROTOCOLS

The course correction component addresses lapses and challenges immediately rather than allowing them to accumulate into abandonment of the entire system. When you notice you've answered no to multiple questions for several days, the system provides specific recovery protocols that get you back on track without starting over from the beginning or engaging in self-criticism that makes resuming practices more difficult.

These recovery protocols include identifying the smallest possible action you can take in each area to reconnect immediately, such as appreciating something you can see from where you're sitting, asking your gut feeling about what to do next, sending a brief message to someone you care about, writing down one thing you learned recently, or taking three deep breaths as an act of self-care.

REFLECT, REVIEW & PLAN

The system also includes reflection questions that help you understand what led to lapses without creating elaborate strategies to prevent them from happening again. Most lapses occur due to temporary circumstances like travel, illness, work deadlines, or family crises that don't require permanent changes to your approach but simply need to be acknowledged as normal life fluctuations that don't invalidate your overall progress.

Monthly reviews provide opportunities to assess which practices are becoming automatic versus which still require conscious effort, which areas are developing most naturally, and what adjustments would make your approach more effective or sustainable. These reviews prevent the system from becoming rigid or outdated as you grow and your circumstances change.

The check-in system also includes planning components that help you prepare for upcoming challenges or opportunities rather than just reacting to whatever happens. If you know you'll be traveling next week, you can adapt your practices to work with limited time and different environments. If you're anticipating a stressful period, you can emphasize self-care practices that will support you through the difficulty.

The system evolves with you as practices become more natural and require less conscious management. After several months, you might shift from daily tracking to weekly reviews, or from yes-or-no questions to more nuanced reflections about quality and depth of engagement. The goal is maintaining accountability and awareness without creating a bureaucratic burden that makes the practices feel like work rather than natural expressions of who you're becoming.

Most importantly, the daily check-in system creates a relationship with yourself based on curiosity and support rather than judgment and criticism. You become interested in your patterns and progress rather than critical of your imperfections, approaching personal development as an ongoing experiment rather than a performance that needs to be perfect to be valuable.

Troubleshooting Challenges and Resistance

Resistance to positive change emerges predictably during any transformation process, not because you don't want to grow but because your psychological and social systems are designed to maintain familiar patterns even when those patterns don't serve your current goals and values. Understanding common forms of resistance and having specific strategies for working with them prevents temporary challenges from derailing your entire effort.

The most common form of resistance appears as sudden loss of motivation around day 10 to 15, when initial enthusiasm fades and practices start feeling routine rather than exciting. This motivational dip happens to everyone and doesn't indicate that the approach isn't working or that you lack discipline. It simply means you're transitioning from inspiration-driven effort to habit-driven consistency, which always feels less energizing than the initial excitement of starting something new.

When motivation drops, the solution is reducing practice intensity rather than increasing it, making your daily requirements so small that you can maintain them even when you don't feel like doing them. Instead of abandoning your gratitude practice when it feels forced, appreciate one thing you can see from wherever you are. Instead of skipping intuitive check-ins when they seem pointless, ask your gut feeling about what to have for lunch. These micro-practices maintain momentum without requiring energy you don't have.

Perfectionism creates resistance by demanding flawless implementation and then using inevitable lapses as evidence that you should abandon the entire effort rather than simply resuming practices after missing a few days. The perfectionist voice argues that if you can't do something perfectly, you shouldn't do it at all, creating all-or-nothing thinking that prevents the gradual progress that actually creates lasting change.

Working with perfectionist resistance involves explicitly giving yourself permission to implement practices imperfectly while still receiving full credit for your efforts. A forced gratitude practice counts just as much as an inspired one. Checking in with your intuition and receiving unclear guidance still builds your capacity for inner awareness. Imperfect engagement with all five key areas creates more transformation than perfect engagement with none of them.

Social resistance often emerges when family members or friends respond to your changes with skepticism, criticism, or subtle sabotage because your growth triggers their own insecurities about areas where they're not developing. People might make jokes about your "self-help phase," question whether you're becoming too serious or spiritual, or create situations that make maintaining your practices more difficult.

Handling social resistance requires maintaining your commitment to growth while avoiding defensive explanations or attempts to convince others that your changes are valuable. You simply continue your practices without making them the focus of conversations or seeking validation from people who aren't ready to support your development. Your consistency and the positive results you experience will speak louder than any explanations you could offer.

Time pressure resistance claims that you don't have enough time for personal development practices, even though the basic G.I.F.T.S. approach requires less than ten minutes daily and integrates into activities you're already doing. This resistance often masks deeper fears about change or concerns that focusing on yourself is selfish when other people need your attention and energy.

Addressing time resistance involves demonstrating through experience that personal development practices actually create more time and energy for other priorities rather than competing with them. When you're operating from gratitude, inner wisdom, strong relationships, applied learning, and self-care, you make better decisions, waste less energy on drama and conflict, and show up more effectively for your responsibilities and relationships.

Identity resistance emerges when new practices conflict with your existing self-concept or when positive changes trigger fear about losing familiar aspects of your personality. You might worry that becoming more grateful will make you naive, that trusting your intuition will make you impractical, or that practicing self-care will make you selfish. These fears reflect concerns about losing parts of yourself that feel essential to who you are.

Working with identity resistance involves recognizing that growth enhances rather than eliminates your core qualities, making you more authentically yourself rather than turning you into someone different. Gratitude doesn't make you naive; it makes you realistically appreciative of what's working while maintaining clear awareness of what needs improvement. Self-care doesn't make you selfish; it ensures you have resources to contribute sustainably to others.

Overwhelm resistance occurs when you try to implement all practices perfectly from the beginning rather than building gradually from simple foundations. This typically happens when you're excited about the potential benefits and want to accelerate the timeline by doing more rather than trusting the process of gradual integration that actually creates lasting change.

Preventing overwhelm requires starting with the absolute minimum effective dose of each practice and increasing intensity only after basic practices feel natural and automatic. It's better to maintain simple practices consistently for months than to implement elaborate systems that you abandon after a few weeks because they require more energy than you can sustain.

Comparison resistance develops when you measure your progress against other people's results or against idealized versions of how you think you should be developing. This comparison creates discouragement and self-criticism that undermines the very practices that would create the growth you're seeking, turning personal development into a competitive performance rather than an individual journey.

Addressing comparison resistance involves focusing on your own baseline rather than other people's achievements, celebrating small improvements in your own experience rather than measuring yourself against external standards. Your gratitude practice only needs to be better than your previous tendency toward complaint and dissatisfaction. Your intuitive development only needs to improve your own decision-making capacity.

Seasonal resistance occurs when life circumstances change in ways that disrupt your established routines, such as travel, illness, work deadlines, or family crises. Instead of adapting practices to new circumstances, many people abandon them entirely and then struggle to resume when conditions return to normal.

Preparing for seasonal resistance involves having modified versions of all practices that can be maintained during challenging periods, even if they're much simpler than your normal routine. Travel versions, sick day versions, and crisis versions of your practices ensure continuity even when your regular schedule gets disrupted, preventing a complete breakdown that often leads to permanent abandonment.

30-Day G.I.F.T.S. Integration

The 30-Day G.I.F.T.S. Integration System provides a systematic approach that transforms accumulated wisdom into lived reality through weekly progression that builds sustainable practices gradually rather than trying to implement everything perfectly from day one. The timeline leverages neuroscience insights about habit formation while providing enough time to work through predictable resistance without creating overwhelming long-term commitments that feel impossible before you start.

The daily check-in system ensures follow-through by tracking completion rather than quality across all five key areas, providing immediate course correction when you drift away from practices while celebrating progress that builds momentum for continued effort. Common challenges and resistance patterns have specific solutions that prevent temporary difficulties from derailing your entire transformation effort.

Your first implementation step is to

- Choose your official start date, marking it on your calendar and preparing your environment to support success rather than hoping motivation will carry you through inevitable obstacles.
- Clear your schedule of non-essential commitments during the first week, and inform supportive family members or friends about it.
- Gather any materials you need for tracking your daily progress. To set up your tracking system using a simple calendar, chart, or notebook where you can record daily yes-or-no responses to the five G.I.F.T.S. questions.
- Choose a consistent time for your daily check-in, preferably in the evening when you can review the entire day's experience and plan any adjustments for tomorrow. Consistency of timing makes the review automatic rather than something you have to remember to do.

Your second step is to define your week one practices using the simplest possible versions that require minimal time and energy while creating meaningful contact with each area.

1. Plan to appreciate three things during existing transition moments.
2. Check in with your intuition before making one decision daily.
3. Have one meaningful interaction with someone you care about.
4. Capture one insight and identify how to apply it.
5. Do one thing that demonstrates self-care.

Write these practices down specifically, rather than keeping them as general intentions, identifying exactly when and how you'll implement each one within your existing daily routine. Make note of what you do to establish habits whenever possible, such as practicing gratitude while drinking your morning coffee or checking in with your intuition before getting out of your car at work.

Your third step is to identify your most likely sources of resistance and prepare specific strategies for working with them before they arise. If you tend toward perfectionism, give yourself explicit permission to implement practices imperfectly while receiving full credit for your efforts. If social resistance is likely, prepare responses to skeptical comments that maintain your commitment without becoming defensive or argumentative.

- Create modified versions of all practices for challenging circumstances such as travel, illness, or work deadlines, ensuring you can maintain some version of your routine regardless of disruptions to your normal schedule. These backup plans prevent the complete breaks that often lead to permanent abandonment when life gets complicated.

Your fourth step is to establish your support system by

- Identifying at least one person who will encourage your growth effort and can provide accountability or encouragement when motivation drops.

This might be a family member, friend, or colleague who shares similar development goals, or simply someone who cares about your wellbeing and will check in on your progress periodically. Consider finding others who want to do this simultaneously, creating mutual support without formal accountability partnerships that might become burdensome if circumstances change. Share your commitment publicly if that provides helpful motivation, or keep it private if external attention creates pressure that interferes with your natural development process.

Your final step is to

- Begin now rather than waiting for perfect conditions or more convenient timing that may never arrive.

- Commit to maintaining your practices for the full 30 days, regardless of how inspired or successful they feel on any particular day.

Treat the process as an experiment in systematic integration rather than a performance that needs to be perfect to be valuable. Remember that consistency matters more than intensity during the establishment period, and that missing occasional days doesn't invalidate your entire effort if you resume practices quickly rather than using lapses as excuses for complete abandonment.

The goal is building the foundation for automatic responses that will continue developing long after the initial implementation period ends, creating lasting transformation that feels natural rather than forced.

By day 30, the G.I.F.T.S. practices won't feel like things you're trying to remember to do. They'll feel like natural expressions of who you're becoming, creating the lived reality of gratitude, intuitive wisdom, meaningful relationships, applied learning, and authentic self-care that transforms not just your daily experience but your fundamental relationship with yourself and your life.

10

WHEN LIFE GETS MESSY

You wake up one morning and realize it's been three weeks since you practiced gratitude with any consistency, two weeks since you checked in with your intuition before making decisions, and you can't remember the last time you had a meaningful conversation with someone you care about. The G.I.F.T.S. practices that felt so natural just a month ago now seem like distant memories, casualties of a work crisis, family emergency, or simply the gradual drift that happens when life gets overwhelming and old patterns reassert themselves.

This moment of recognition triggers a familiar cascade of self-criticism and discouragement that makes resuming your practices feel even more difficult than starting them originally. Your inner voice launches into a litany of judgment about your lack of discipline, your inability to maintain positive changes, and your tendency to abandon good intentions when they're needed most. The shame and frustration create additional resistance that turns a simple lapse into what feels like evidence of fundamental personal failure.

But this moment is not a failure; it's a predictable part of any genuine transformation process, and how you handle it determines whether temporary setbacks become permanent abandonment or valuable learning experiences that strengthen your capacity for sustainable growth. The G.I.F.T.S. Recovery Protocol provides systematic approaches for getting back on track that treat lapses as normal rather than catastrophic, information rather than indictment, and opportunities for deeper integration rather than reasons for self-attack.

The recovery process operates on the understanding that lasting change happens through cycles of engagement, lapse, and renewal rather than linear progress toward perfect consistency. Every person who successfully integrates new patterns into their life goes through multiple cycles of practicing, drifting, recognizing the drift, and recommitting with deeper understanding of what supports their growth versus what undermines it.

Perfectionism Kills Transformation

Perfectionism masquerades as high standards and commitment to excellence, but it actually represents one of the most destructive forces working against sustainable personal transformation because it creates impossible expectations that guarantee failure and then uses that inevitable failure as evidence that you should abandon your efforts entirely rather than simply adjusting your approach based on what you've learned.

The perfectionist mindset treats any deviation from ideal implementation as complete failure rather than recognizing that real-world application of growth practices necessarily involves adaptation, interruption, and gradual refinement based on changing circumstances and deepening understanding. When you demand flawless consistency from yourself, you're essentially requiring that you transcend normal human limitations and life complexities that affect everyone's ability to maintain new patterns perfectly.

This all-or-nothing thinking creates a psychological trap where missing practices for a few days becomes interpreted as evidence that you lack the discipline or commitment necessary for lasting change, leading to abandonment of approaches that were actually working well before the temporary interruption occurred. Instead of treating lapses as normal fluctuations in any learning process, perfectionism transforms them into character indictments that justify giving up entirely.

The perfectionist voice argues that if you can't maintain practices consistently, you shouldn't bother trying at all, creating false choices between perfect implementation and complete abandonment that ignore the reality that most beneficial changes happen through imperfect but persistent engagement over time rather than through flawless execution from the beginning. This binary thinking prevents the gradual progress that actually creates lasting transformation.

Perfectionism also creates unsustainable pressure that makes practices feel like performance evaluations rather than supportive tools for enhancing your life experience. When every day becomes a test of whether you're disciplined enough to maintain your gratitude practice, wise enough to trust your intuition consistently, or caring enough to prioritize relationships appropriately, the practices become sources of stress rather than resources for managing life's challenges more effectively.

This performance pressure transforms natural learning processes into anxiety-provoking obligations that your nervous system begins to resist because they've become associated with judgment and potential failure rather than growth and self-care. What started as practices designed to improve your wellbeing becomes additional sources of self-criticism that actually decrease your overall life satisfaction and emotional stability.

The perfectionist approach also ignores the reality that different life seasons require different levels of engagement with growth practices, and that adapting your approach to current circumstances demonstrates wisdom rather than weakness. During periods of crisis, illness, major life transitions, or unusual stress, maintaining simplified versions of your practices shows more self-awareness and sustainability than trying to force normal routines that don't match your current capacity.

Research on habit formation and behavior change consistently shows that people who maintain practices long-term are those who develop flexible approaches that can adapt to changing circumstances rather than rigid systems that collapse when life becomes unpredictable. The ability to scale practices up or down based on available time and energy creates resilience that allows continued engagement even during challenging periods.

Perfectionism prevents this adaptive flexibility by creating shame around any modifications to ideal implementation, making you feel like you're cheating or giving up when you adjust practices to match your current reality. This shame keeps you stuck in cycles of attempting perfect execution, failing to maintain it consistently, feeling guilty about the failure, and abandoning the practices entirely rather than finding sustainable middle ground.

The antidote to perfectionism involves embracing what researchers call "good enough" approaches that prioritize consistency over intensity, progress over perfection, and sustainable engagement over impressive short-term results. When you give yourself permission to implement practices imperfectly while still receiving full credit for your efforts, you create conditions where long-term transformation becomes possible because you're working with human nature rather than against it.

This good enough approach recognizes that a simple gratitude practice maintained for months creates more transformation than an elaborate appreciation routine that gets abandoned after two weeks because it requires more time and energy than you can sustain consistently. Imperfect engagement with all five G.I.F.T.S. key areas produces better results than perfect engagement with none of them.

The shift from perfectionist to sustainable thinking also involves redefining success as the ability to recover quickly from lapses rather than the ability to avoid them entirely. When you measure your progress by how fast you get back on track after missing practices rather than by how consistently you avoid missing them, you develop resilience and self-compassion that support long-term growth rather than short-term performance.

This recovery-focused definition of success acknowledges that life will inevitably present challenges that disrupt even the best-established routines, and that your capacity to resume beneficial practices after interruptions matters more than your ability to prevent interruptions from occurring. Every time you restart your practices after a lapse, you're strengthening the neural pathways that make future recovery faster and easier.

The 24-Hour Recovery Rule

The 24-Hour Recovery Rule provides a specific protocol for getting back on track within one day of noticing you've drifted away from your G.I.F.T.S. practices, preventing the all-or-nothing thinking that turns temporary slips into permanent abandonment of your growth efforts. This rule operates on the principle that immediate action creates momentum while delayed response allows resistance and self-criticism to build barriers that make resuming practices increasingly difficult.

The rule begins with recognition rather than judgment when you notice you've been off track, treating the awareness itself as a positive development rather than evidence of failure. The moment you realize you haven't been practicing gratitude, checking in with your intuition, connecting meaningfully with others, applying wisdom, or caring for yourself appropriately, you've already taken the first step toward recovery by becoming conscious of patterns that were operating automatically.

This recognition phase involves acknowledging what happened without elaborate analysis of why it happened or complex strategies for preventing it from happening again. Most lapses occur due to temporary circumstances like increased work demands, family situations, travel, illness, or seasonal stress that don't require permanent changes to your approach but simply need to be accepted as normal life fluctuations that affect everyone's ability to maintain consistent routines.

The immediate action component requires taking one small step in each of the five G.I.F.T.S. key areas within 24 hours of recognizing the lapse, regardless of how unmotivated or resistant you feel about resuming your practices. These actions need to be so simple that you can complete them even when you're busy, stressed, or doubting the value of the entire approach, creating momentum without requiring the energy or enthusiasm that might not be available during recovery periods.

For gratitude, the 24-hour action might involve appreciating three things you can see from wherever you're sitting right now, focusing on immediate sensory experiences rather than abstract blessings that might feel forced when you're not in an appreciative mood. The warmth of sunlight through a window, the comfort of your chair, or the convenience of having clean water available provide concrete foundations for genuine appreciation that don't require emotional stretching.

Your intuitive intention recovery action involves asking your gut feeling about one small decision you need to make within the next few hours, such as what to eat for your next meal, which route to take somewhere, or how to spend a brief break in your schedule. These low-stakes decisions provide practice for accessing inner guidance without the pressure of major life choices that might feel overwhelming when you're already feeling disconnected from your wisdom.

Family and friends connection recovery requires one meaningful interaction within 24 hours, whether through sending an appreciative message to someone you care about, having a brief but present conversation with a family member, or simply making eye contact and smiling at people you encounter throughout your day. The goal is creating genuine human connection rather than just going through social motions.

Treasured wisdom recovery involves capturing one insight from your recent experience and identifying how you could apply it immediately, whether that insight comes from a conversation, a challenge you've been navigating, something you've read, or simply reflection on what you've learned about yourself during the period when you were off track. This application needs to be specific and actionable rather than general or theoretical.

Self-love and care recovery requires doing one thing within 24 hours that demonstrates kindness toward yourself, whether through speaking to yourself more gently about the lapse itself, meeting a basic need you've been ignoring, or simply taking three conscious breaths as an act of self-compassion. This action should feel nurturing rather than obligatory, providing genuine care rather than checking off a requirement.

The rule emphasizes completion over quality during the recovery period, giving you full credit for any engagement with each area regardless of how inspired, successful, or transformative the actions feel. The goal is rebuilding momentum and connection with your practices rather than creating profound experiences or catching up on everything you missed while you were off track.

This completion focus prevents the perfectionist thinking that often sabotages recovery efforts by demanding that resumption be as elaborate or consistent as your practices were before the lapse occurred. You don't need to return immediately to your previous level of engagement. You just need to take small steps that reestablish contact with each area and remind your nervous system what these practices feel like.

The 24-hour timeframe creates urgency that prevents procrastination while being reasonable enough that you can almost always find ways to complete the recovery actions regardless of how busy or challenging your current circumstances might be. Longer timeframes allow resistance to build and make resuming practices feel increasingly difficult, while shorter timeframes might not provide enough flexibility for complex schedules.

The rule also includes specific language for talking to yourself during the recovery process that maintains self-compassion while creating account-ability for getting back on track. Instead of criticizing yourself for the lapse, you might say "I notice I've been away from my practices for a while, and that's completely normal. I'm ready to reconnect with what supports my growth, starting with small steps today."

This supportive internal dialogue prevents the shame spiral that often makes recovery more difficult by treating you as an ally in your growth process rather than an adversary who needs to be controlled or punished. When you approach recovery with curiosity and kindness rather than judgment and force, your nervous system cooperates rather than resists the process of resuming beneficial practices.

The rule recognizes that recovery might need to happen multiple times throughout your growth journey, and that becoming skilled at getting back on track quickly is more valuable than trying to prevent all future lapses through perfect consistency. Each time you successfully implement the 24-hour recovery protocol, you're building confidence in your ability to maintain long-term growth despite temporary interruptions.

Adapting G.I.F.T.S. During Crisis

High-stress periods and personal crises create conditions where your normal G.I.F.T.S. practices might feel impossible or inappropriate, but these are exactly the times when you need the emotional stability and inner resources that these practices provide most desperately. The key is adapting your approach to match your current capacity rather than abandoning the practices entirely when you need their support most urgently.

Crisis adaptation operates on the principle that maintaining simplified versions of your practices provides more benefit than perfect execution of elaborate routines that become impossible to sustain when your energy and attention are consumed by immediate challenges. During these periods, the goal shifts from growth and development to stability and basic self-care, using G.I.F.T.S. practices as anchors rather than improvement projects.

Stress-period gratitude focuses on immediate, concrete experiences rather than abstract appreciation for life circumstances that might feel overwhelming or inappropriate when you're dealing with serious difficulties. Instead of trying to feel grateful for challenges as growth opportunities, you might appreciate the warmth of coffee in your hands, the fact that you have shelter during a storm, or the kindness of one person who offered support during your crisis.

This concrete gratitude provides emotional grounding without requiring you to find meaning or silver linings in genuinely difficult situations that deserve acknowledgment as painful rather than reframing as blessings in disguise. You can appreciate small comforts and supports while fully acknowledging that your overall circumstances are challenging and deserve compassionate attention rather than forced positivity.

Crisis gratitude might also include appreciation for your own resilience and coping efforts, recognizing that you're handling a difficult situation as well as anyone could, rather than criticizing yourself for not managing stress perfectly. "I appreciate that I'm doing my best in a really hard situation" provides self-support without denying the reality of your challenges or demanding that you feel grateful for experiences that are genuinely difficult.

Intuitive intention during high-stress periods involves checking in with your inner wisdom about immediate needs and next steps rather than long-term decision-making that might feel overwhelming when you're already dealing with crisis management. Your gut feelings about whether you need rest or activity, solitude or connection, help or independence can guide moment-to-moment choices that support your wellbeing during challenging times.

This crisis intuition often becomes clearer than usual because stress strips away social expectations and mental complications, allowing you to access basic wisdom about what your system needs for stability and recovery. Your body and emotions provide direct feedback about what helps versus what adds to your stress load, giving you reliable guidance for navigating immediate circumstances even when long-term planning feels impossible.

You might ask simplified intuitive questions like "What do I need right now?" or "What would help me get through the next few hours?" rather than complex decision-making processes that require energy you don't have available during crisis periods. These basic check-ins help you make choices that support your capacity to handle challenges rather than depleting your already limited resources.

Family and friends connection during a crisis involves accepting support rather than trying to maintain your usual role as caregiver or problem-solver for others. This might mean allowing people to help you with practical tasks, being honest about your emotional state rather than protecting others from your difficulties, or simply staying in contact with supportive people even when you don't have energy to give back equally.

Crisis connection also includes setting boundaries with people who increase your stress through criticism, unsolicited advice, or emotional demands that exceed your current capacity. During high-stress periods, you have permission to limit contact with relationships that drain your energy and prioritize connections that provide genuine support and understanding without requiring you to manage their reactions to your situation.

You might maintain connection through brief text messages rather than long phone calls, accept help with tasks rather than trying to handle everything independently, or simply let trusted people know you're going through a difficult time without feeling obligated to provide detailed explanations or reassurance that you'll be fine soon.

Treasured wisdom during a crisis focuses on using knowledge and insights you've already gained rather than trying to learn new approaches or collect additional information when your processing capacity is already overwhelmed by immediate circumstances. This might involve applying basic stress management techniques you know work for you, using communication skills you've developed in previous difficult conversations, or drawing on spiritual or philosophical resources that have provided comfort during past challenges.

Crisis wisdom also includes recognizing when you need professional support beyond what you can provide for yourself through personal development practices. Sometimes the wisest application of your accumulated learning is knowing when to seek help from therapists, medical professionals, financial advisors, or other experts who can provide specialized assistance that matches the specific challenges you're facing.

You might also apply wisdom about your own patterns and needs during stress, using previous crisis experiences to guide current choices about pacing, support-seeking, and self-care that helped you navigate similar situations successfully in the past. This self-knowledge becomes particularly valuable during a crisis because it provides tested strategies rather than experimental approaches.

Self-love and care during high-stress periods involves meeting basic needs and treating yourself with extra gentleness rather than maintaining elaborate self-care routines that might feel impossible when you're dealing with crisis management. This might mean prioritizing sleep over exercise, accepting help with household tasks, eating simple but nourishing foods, or giving yourself permission to feel whatever emotions are arising without trying to manage them perfectly.

Crisis self-care also includes protecting yourself from additional stressors that aren't directly related to your immediate situation, such as limiting news consumption that increases anxiety, avoiding social media that triggers comparison or overwhelm, or postponing non-essential decisions that would require mental energy you need for handling your current challenges.

The most important aspect of crisis self-care involves speaking to yourself with the same compassion you would offer to anyone else facing similar difficulties, recognizing that your current struggles are temporary even when they feel overwhelming, and trusting that you have the capacity to get through this period even if you can't see exactly how that will happen right now.

Adapted G.I.F.T.S. practices during a crisis provide stability and support without adding to your stress load, serving as anchors that keep you connected to resources for resilience and recovery rather than improvement projects that require energy you don't have available. These simplified practices can be maintained with minimal effort while still providing the emotional grounding and inner connection that help you navigate challenging periods with greater stability and self-compassion.

Using Setbacks as Stepping Stones

Setbacks and lapses in your G.I.F.T.S. practices contain valuable information about your patterns, triggers, and needs that can strengthen your approach and deepen your self-understanding when you learn to extract wisdom from struggles rather than just enduring them as evidence of personal failure. This learning process transforms what feels like regression into opportunities for developing more sustainable and personalized approaches to growth that work with your actual life rather than against it.

The information extraction process begins with a curious examination of what led to the setback rather than a judgmental analysis of failure. Most lapses occur due to predictable patterns that can be identified and addressed once you understand the specific conditions that make maintaining practices more difficult versus the circumstances that support natural engagement with growth activities.

You might discover that you maintain practices well during normal weeks but abandon them completely when traveling, that you're consistent with morning routines but struggle with evening practices, that relationship stress triggers abandonment of self-care, or that work deadlines cause you to prioritize productivity over presence and wisdom. These patterns provide specific information for designing approaches that work with your tendencies rather than fighting against them.

Environmental factors often play larger roles in setbacks than personal discipline issues, revealing opportunities for creating better support systems that make positive choices easier rather than relying on willpower to overcome challenging circumstances. If you notice that you skip gratitude practice when your phone is the first thing you see upon waking, the solution involves changing your environment rather than trying to develop stronger discipline about ignoring digital distractions.

Similarly, if you discover that you abandon intuitive check-ins during busy work periods, you might need to attach these practices to activities that happen automatically during stressful times rather than expecting yourself to remember new behaviors when your attention is consumed by urgent demands. Environmental design often provides more sustainable solutions than personal motivation for maintaining beneficial practices.

Energy management patterns revealed through setback analysis help you understand when you have capacity for growth practices versus when you need to focus on basic maintenance and recovery. Some people maintain practices well when they're busy but abandon them during periods of low energy or depression. Others can sustain routines during calm periods but drop everything when life becomes overwhelming.

Understanding your personal energy patterns allows you to create different versions of your practices that match your actual capacity during various life seasons rather than expecting yourself to maintain the same level of engagement regardless of circumstances. Having simplified practices for low-energy periods and expanded approaches for high-capacity times creates flexibility that prevents complete abandonment during challenging phases.

Social and relationship dynamics often influence setbacks in ways that become clear only through reflection on what was happening in your connections with others when you drifted away from practices. Some people abandon self-care when relationships become demanding, while others stop practicing gratitude when they're angry with family members, or discontinue applying wisdom when they're trying to please others who don't value personal development.

Recognizing these relationship patterns helps you understand how your growth practices interact with your social environment and identify ways to maintain beneficial behaviors even when others aren't supportive or when relationship challenges consume your emotional energy. This might involve setting boundaries that protect your practice time or finding ways to adapt approaches that don't trigger resistance from people who feel threatened by your changes.

Seasonal patterns, periods, or cycles often emerge through setback analysis, revealing that lapses tend to occur during specific times of year, particular phases of work or family cycles, or in response to recurring stressors that appear predictably in your life. Understanding these cycles allows you to prepare for challenging periods rather than being surprised by them and abandoning practices when you need them most.

You might discover that you struggle with practices during winter months when daylight is limited, during back-to-school seasons when family schedules become chaotic, or during anniversary periods of losses or traumas that affect your emotional stability. Anticipating these challenging times allows you to modify your approach proactively rather than reactively abandoning practices when difficulties arise.

The learning process also includes identifying what helps you recover quickly from setbacks versus what keeps you stuck in cycles of abandonment and self-criticism. Some people recover best through gentle self-compassion and gradual re-engagement, while others need firm accountability and immediate action to prevent temporary lapses from becoming permanent abandonment.

Understanding your personal recovery style helps you develop specific protocols for getting back on track that match your psychological makeup rather than following generic advice that might not work for your particular combination of personality traits and life circumstances. This personalized approach to recovery makes setbacks feel less threatening because you know exactly how to handle them when they occur.

Setbacks also reveal hidden perfectionist expectations and all-or-nothing thinking patterns that sabotage long-term success by creating unrealistic standards for what constitutes successful practice maintenance. When you examine why missing practices for a few days led to complete abandonment, you often discover underlying beliefs about consistency that need to be adjusted to support sustainable growth rather than perfect performance.

This examination might reveal that you expect yourself to maintain practices with machine-like consistency rather than human flexibility, that you interpret any deviation from ideal implementation as complete failure, or that you believe growth should happen without interruption rather than through cycles of engagement and integration. Adjusting these beliefs creates more realistic expectations that support long-term development.

The wisdom extraction process transforms setbacks from sources of shame and discouragement into valuable feedback that improves your approach and deepens your understanding of what supports your growth versus what undermines it. Each lapse becomes a learning opportunity that strengthens your capacity for sustainable transformation rather than evidence that you're incapable of lasting positive change.

This learning-focused approach to setbacks also builds resilience and self-trust because you develop confidence in your ability to recover from difficulties and extract value from challenging experiences rather than being derailed by them. When setbacks become stepping stones rather than roadblocks, your growth process becomes more robust and sustainable over time.

Recovery Implementation Process

Perfectionism kills transformation by creating impossible expectations that guarantee failure and then using that inevitable failure as evidence for complete abandonment rather than course correction and continued engagement. The ability to recover quickly from setbacks matters more than the ability to avoid them entirely, and lapses contain valuable information about your patterns and needs that can strengthen your approach when you learn to extract wisdom rather than just endure struggle.

The 24-Hour Recovery Rule provides immediate action steps for getting back on track within one day of noticing drift, preventing temporary slips from becoming permanent abandonment through simple reconnection actions in all five G.I.F.T.S. key areas. During crisis and high-stress periods, adapting practices to match your current capacity provides more benefit than perfect execution of elaborate routines that become impossible to sustain when energy is consumed by immediate challenges.

Your first implementation step is to write down your personal definition of successful practice maintenance that emphasizes recovery speed over perfect consistency, giving yourself full credit for getting back on track quickly rather than measuring success only by unbroken streaks of ideal implementation. Create language like "I measure my success by how quickly I resume beneficial practices after life interrupts them" rather than "I must maintain practices perfectly to be successful."

Identify the specific thoughts and beliefs that typically lead you to abandon practices entirely after missing them for a few days, such as "If I can't do it perfectly, I shouldn't do it at all" or "Missing practices proves I lack discipline." Write down more realistic alternatives like "Imperfect engagement creates more transformation than perfect abandonment" and "Recovery is a skill that improves with practice."

Your second step is to create your personal 24-Hour Recovery Protocol by identifying the smallest possible action you can take in each G.I.F.T.S. area when you notice you've been off track. These actions should require less than one minute each and be doable regardless of your circumstances, energy level, or motivation. Write these recovery actions down and keep them easily accessible for when you need them.

For gratitude, this might be appreciating three things you can see from wherever you are. For intuitive intention, asking your gut feeling about what to do next. For relationships, sending a brief appreciative message to someone you care about. For wisdom, writing down one thing you learned recently. For self-care, taking three conscious breaths or drinking a glass of water mindfully.

Your third step is to design crisis-adapted versions of all five practices that can be maintained during high-stress periods when your normal routines become impossible. These simplified approaches should provide emotional stability and support without adding to your stress load, serving as anchors rather than improvement projects during challenging times.

Crisis gratitude might focus on immediate sensory experiences like warmth or comfort rather than abstract appreciation. Crisis intuition might involve asking "What do I need right now?" rather than complex decision-making. Crisis connection might mean accepting help rather than trying to support others. Crisis wisdom might involve using strategies that you already know work rather than learning new approaches. Crisis self-care might prioritize basic needs like sleep and nutrition over elaborate wellness routines.

Your fourth step is to conduct a setback analysis of your most recent lapse in practices by examining what led to the drift without judgment or self-criticism, looking for patterns in timing, circumstances, energy levels, relationship dynamics, or environmental factors that made maintaining practices more difficult. Use this information to identify specific adjustments that would make future lapses less likely or shorter in duration.

Ask yourself questions like:

"What was happening in my life when I stopped practicing?"

"What environmental factors made practices feel more difficult?"

"What energy or emotional patterns preceded the lapse?"

"What relationship dynamics influenced my ability to maintain growth activities?"

Use the answers to create proactive strategies rather than just hoping to avoid similar circumstances in the future.

Your final step is to establish a weekly recovery review where you assess whether you've been maintaining practices consistently or need to implement your 24-hour recovery protocol, treating this check-in as routine maintenance rather than crisis intervention. During this review, celebrate successful recoveries from previous lapses and adjust your approaches based on what you're learning about your patterns and needs.

Use this weekly review to identify early warning signs that you're beginning to drift away from practices before complete abandonment occurs, such as feeling less motivated, skipping practices occasionally, or experiencing increased stress without using your support tools. Early intervention prevents minor drifts from becoming major setbacks that require more intensive recovery efforts.

Track your recovery skills using questions like "How quickly did I get back on track after my last lapse?" and "What did I learn about my patterns from recent setbacks?" rather than only measuring perfect consistency. This approach builds confidence in your ability to maintain long-term growth despite temporary interruptions while developing the resilience that makes sustainable transformation possible.

11

DEEPENING YOUR PRACTICE

After you've been practicing the G.I.F.T.S. method for several months, you will notice that something fundamental has shifted in how you move through your days. Gratitude will no longer feel like something you have to remember to practice. It emerges naturally when you notice the steam rising from your morning coffee or catch your partner laughing at something on their phone. Your intuition speaks more clearly now, offering guidance that you trust enough to follow even when it contradicts your logical analysis. Your relationships feel more authentic and nourishing because you've learned to show up with presence rather than distraction.

The wisdom you've been collecting from books and experiences actually gets applied now instead of just accumulating in your mental library, and you treat yourself with a kindness that would have felt foreign six months ago. These changes didn't happen through dramatic transformation or perfect implementation. They emerged gradually through consistent engagement with practices that have become woven into who you are, rather than tasks you manage through willpower.

This integration creates a solid foundation, but it also opens the door to deeper possibilities that weren't accessible when you were still learning the basics. Advanced G.I.F.T.S. practice involves expanding beyond personal transformation into leadership, legacy, and service that emerges naturally from the fullness you've created rather than from obligation or external expectations. You're ready to explore what becomes possible when gratitude, intuitive wisdom, meaningful relationships, applied learning, and self-compassion operate as an integrated way of being rather than separate practices you maintain.

The advanced practices in this chapter build on your established foundation without requiring you to abandon what's already working well. Instead, they represent natural evolution of capacities you've already developed, showing you how to deepen your experience while expanding your positive influence in ways that feel authentic rather than forced, sustainable rather than depleting, and joyful rather than burdensome.

Recognizing When You're Ready to Go Deeper

The readiness for advanced G.I.F.T.S. practices reveals itself through subtle but unmistakable signs that indicate your basic practices have become automatic responses rather than conscious efforts, creating space for deeper exploration without abandoning the foundation you've worked so carefully to establish. These signs emerge gradually and might not be obvious until you reflect specifically on how your relationship with the practices has evolved over time.

The clearest indicator of readiness appears when you notice that skipping practices feels unnatural rather than requiring discipline to maintain them. When gratitude becomes your default response to both positive and challenging experiences, when checking in with your intuition feels as automatic as looking both ways before crossing the street, when meaningful connection with others happens naturally rather than through conscious effort, you've moved beyond practice maintenance into integrated living.

This shift from effortful practice to natural expression typically occurs after three to six months of consistent engagement, though the timeline varies based on your starting point, life circumstances, and depth of commitment to the integration process. The key indicator isn't perfect consistency but rather the sense that these ways of being feel like authentic expressions of your personality rather than behaviors you're imposing on yourself through willpower or external motivation.

Another sign of readiness involves noticing that your practices continue to develop and deepen without conscious effort to improve them. Your gratitude naturally expands to include appreciation for difficulties and challenges as opportunities for growth. Your intuitive capacity becomes more sophisticated, providing guidance not just about personal decisions but about how to contribute positively to situations involving others. Your relationships deepen as you become more comfortable with vulnerability and authentic communication.

This organic development happens because integrated practices create their own momentum for growth rather than remaining static techniques that you apply mechanically. When gratitude becomes part of your identity, it naturally seeks expression in increasingly subtle and comprehensive ways. When trusting your inner wisdom becomes automatic, that wisdom becomes more accessible and reliable because you're no longer fighting against it with doubt and analysis.

You're also ready for advanced practice when you begin experiencing what researchers call "broaden and build" effects, where your established practices create expanding capacities that extend beyond the original five key areas. Your gratitude practice enhances your creativity and problem-solving abilities. Your intuitive development improves your leadership and communication skills. Your relationship focus increases your capacity for empathy and service to others.

These expanding benefits indicate that your practices have created positive changes in your nervous system, cognitive patterns, and emotional regulation that support enhanced functioning across all areas of your life rather than just the specific domains you've been working on directly. This systemic improvement suggests you're ready to explore how your personal transformation can serve purposes larger than individual fulfillment.

The readiness for advanced practice also appears through increased comfort with uncertainty and complexity rather than needing simple, clear guidelines for every situation. You've developed enough trust in your integrated approach that you can adapt practices to new circumstances without losing confidence in their effectiveness. You can modify your gratitude practice for different cultural contexts, apply your intuitive wisdom to professional situations, and maintain authentic relationships even when others don't share your commitment to presence and vulnerability.

This adaptive flexibility indicates that you understand the underlying principles behind the practices rather than just following surface-level instructions, which allows you to maintain the essence of your approach while adjusting the expression to match changing circumstances and opportunities for growth. You've moved from rule-following to principle-guided living that can respond creatively to novel situations.

Another indicator involves noticing that other people are drawn to the qualities you're embodying and begin asking about your approach to life challenges, relationship difficulties, or personal growth. When your way of being naturally inspires curiosity and interest from others, you're demonstrating the kind of integrated transformation that creates positive influence without conscious effort to teach or convince anyone of anything.

This natural attractiveness of your embodied practices suggests that you're ready to explore how your personal development can serve others not through preaching or advice-giving but through authentic modeling of what becomes possible when someone consistently applies wisdom principles to their daily experience. Your life becomes a demonstration of integrated growth rather than just a personal improvement project.

You're ready for advanced practice when you feel genuinely grateful for your challenges and setbacks as well as your successes and blessings, not because you've convinced yourself that everything happens for a reason but because you've experienced directly how difficulties contribute to your growth and deepen your capacity for compassion toward others who face similar struggles.

This mature gratitude includes appreciation for your own imperfections and ongoing areas of development rather than only acknowledging what you've mastered or achieved. You can feel simultaneously grateful for how far you've come and excited about continued growth without the dissatisfaction or self-criticism that characterized your earlier relationship with personal development.

The final indicator of readiness involves experiencing what spiritual traditions call "effortless effort" where maintaining your practices and living according to your principles feels natural and energizing rather than disciplined and depleting. You're no longer swimming against the current of your conditioning but flowing with patterns that support your highest expression while requiring minimal conscious management to maintain.

This effortless quality doesn't mean you never encounter challenges or resistance, but rather that you have reliable ways of working with difficulties that don't require abandoning your principles or reverting to old patterns that no longer serve you. You've developed enough skill and integration that maintaining your growth orientation feels sustainable rather than exhausting, creating the foundation for deeper exploration and expanded service.

Advanced Gratitude

Advanced gratitude transcends the personal benefits of appreciation practices to become a comprehensive philosophy that influences how you interpret all experiences, respond to challenges, and contribute to the wellbeing of others around you. This evolution transforms gratitude from something you do during designated practice times into a lens through which you view reality that creates unshakeable resilience and joy regardless of external circumstances.

The foundation of advanced gratitude involves recognizing appreciation as a choice about how to interpret your experience rather than a response that depends on having obviously positive things to feel grateful for. This shift moves you beyond conditional gratitude that requires good circumstances to circumstantial gratitude that can find meaning and value even in difficult situations without denying their genuine challenges or forcing false positivity.

This philosophical approach doesn't minimize real problems or suggest that you should feel grateful for harmful experiences, but rather develops your capacity to find elements worth appreciating even during periods when your overall circumstances feel challenging or overwhelming. You might appreciate your own courage in facing difficulties, the support you receive from others during hard times, or the growth that emerges from navigating complex situations.

Advanced gratitude also includes appreciation for the full spectrum of human experience rather than only acknowledging positive emotions and pleasant events. You develop the capacity to feel grateful for your ability to feel sadness because it indicates the depth of your love, to appreciate anger because it reveals your values and boundaries, and to value anxiety because it demonstrates your care about outcomes that matter to you.

This emotional inclusivity creates a more stable foundation for appreciation because it doesn't depend on maintaining positive feelings or avoiding negative ones. Instead, it recognizes all emotions as valuable information about your inner world and your relationship with your environment, worthy of appreciation for the guidance and richness they provide to your human experience.

The advanced practice extends gratitude beyond personal benefits to include appreciation for your ability to contribute positively to others and to participate in the larger web of relationships and community that supports all life. You become grateful not just for what you receive but for what you can give, not just for how you're supported but for how you can provide support, not just for your own growth but for your capacity to encourage growth in others.

This contributory gratitude naturally leads to increased generosity and service because appreciation for your ability to make a positive difference creates motivation to exercise that capacity more fully. When you feel genuinely grateful for your skills, resources, and opportunities to help others, using those gifts feels like natural expression of appreciation rather than obligation or duty imposed from outside.

Advanced gratitude practice also involves developing appreciation for the interconnected nature of existence that reveals how your wellbeing depends on countless seen and unseen contributions from other people, natural systems, and cultural inheritances that make your life possible. This recognition creates humility and wonder that counteracts the individualistic thinking that can develop when personal development becomes too focused on self-improvement rather than mutual flourishing.

You begin to appreciate the farmers who grew your food, the workers who built your home, the teachers who shared knowledge that shapes your thinking, the ancestors whose struggles and wisdom created the freedoms and opportunities you enjoy, and the natural systems that provide the air, water, and climate that sustain your life. This expanded awareness creates gratitude that connects you to the larger community of life rather than isolating you in personal appreciation practices.

The philosophical dimension of advanced gratitude includes recognizing appreciation as a form of prayer or spiritual practice that connects you to something larger than your individual concerns and preferences. Whether you understand this connection in religious, spiritual, or secular terms, gratitude becomes a way of acknowledging the mystery and gift of existence itself rather than just cataloging personal benefits.

This spiritual aspect of gratitude creates what many traditions call "reverence for life" that influences how you treat other people, animals, plants, and the environment because you recognize everything as part of the same interconnected system that deserves appreciation and care. Your gratitude practice becomes inseparable from your ethics and your commitment to contributing positively to the world.

Advanced gratitude also involves sharing appreciation in ways that inspire and uplift others without becoming preachy or imposing your perspective on people who aren't interested in gratitude practices. You learn to express appreciation authentically and specifically in ways that help others feel seen and valued while modeling the kind of positive attention that creates more gratitude in your shared environment.

This generous expression of gratitude might involve acknowledging people's contributions in ways that help them recognize their own value, expressing appreciation for beauty and goodness in ways that help others notice what's wonderful around them, or responding to challenges with the kind of grace and perspective that demonstrates gratitude's power without explicitly teaching about it.

The advanced practice includes using gratitude as a tool for social healing and community building by focusing appreciation on qualities and contributions that bring people together rather than differences that create division. You might express gratitude for the diversity of perspectives that enriches your community, for the different strengths that various people contribute to shared projects, or for the common hopes and values that unite people despite surface-level disagreements.

This unifying approach to gratitude helps create more harmonious relationships and communities because appreciation naturally highlights what's working and what's valuable rather than focusing attention on problems and conflicts that can dominate group dynamics when gratitude isn't actively cultivated as a shared practice.

Advanced gratitude ultimately becomes a way of participating in what some traditions call "the great thanksgiving," an ongoing recognition and celebration of the gift of existence that includes both joy and sorrow, success and failure, birth and death as part of the magnificent complexity of being alive in relationship with others in a world that constantly offers opportunities for wonder, learning, and love.

Intuitive Leadership from Inner Wisdom

Intuitive leadership represents the natural evolution of personal intuitive development into the capacity to guide major life decisions and influence others through wisdom that emerges from integrated inner knowing rather than purely analytical thinking or external authority. This advanced application transforms your relationship with uncertainty and complexity while developing your ability to navigate situations where complete information isn't available and traditional decision-making approaches prove inadequate.

The foundation of intuitive leadership involves trusting your inner guidance for decisions that significantly impact your life direction, career choices, relationship commitments, and major transitions that require you to act on incomplete information while accepting responsibility for outcomes that can't be predicted or controlled through logical analysis alone. These high-stakes decisions provide the testing ground where intuitive capacity either proves its reliability or reveals areas where further development is needed.

This trust develops gradually through successful application of inner wisdom to increasingly important choices, building a track record that demonstrates the practical value of intuitive guidance for navigating complex real-world situations. You learn to distinguish between fear-based mental noise and authentic inner knowing by observing which internal signals lead to outcomes that align with your deeper values and long-term wellbeing.

Advanced intuitive decision-making integrates inner wisdom with practical analysis rather than replacing logical thinking with gut feelings, creating a comprehensive approach that draws on both analytical intelligence and intuitive insight to make choices that satisfy both rational assessment and deeper knowing. This integration prevents the common mistake of abandoning critical thinking in favor of following every impulse or emotional reaction.

The integration process involves using intuitive guidance to identify which options deserve detailed analysis while using logical thinking to work out practical implementation of directions that feel right at a deeper level. Your inner wisdom might indicate that a career change aligns with your authentic path while your analytical mind works out the financial planning and timeline that makes the transition possible without creating unnecessary hardship.

Intuitive leadership also involves recognizing when situations require immediate action based on inner knowing versus when they benefit from extended reflection and analysis. Some decisions need to be made quickly based on gut feelings because the window of opportunity won't remain open long enough for complete analysis, while others deserve careful consideration because the consequences of poor choices would be difficult to reverse.

This discernment about timing becomes crucial for effective leadership because it allows you to respond appropriately to different types of situations rather than applying the same decision-making process regardless of context. Emergency situations might require immediate action based on inner knowing, while strategic planning might benefit from combining intuitive direction with detailed analysis and consultation with others.

The leadership dimension emerges when your capacity for intuitive decision-making begins influencing others who recognize the quality of outcomes you create through trusting inner wisdom. People start seeking your perspective on their own difficult decisions because they observe that you navigate uncertainty with unusual clarity and confidence, creating results that demonstrate the practical value of integrated decision-making.

This natural authority develops through demonstration rather than self-promotion, as others notice that your choices consistently align with your stated values while producing outcomes that serve not just your personal interests but the wellbeing of everyone involved in the situations you influence. Your decision-making style becomes attractive to others because it combines wisdom with practical effectiveness.

Intuitive leadership includes the capacity to sense what groups and organizations need for optimal functioning even when those needs aren't explicitly stated or consciously recognized by the people involved. You might intuitively recognize that a team needs more creative freedom, that an organization requires clearer communication about values and direction, or that a community would benefit from increased opportunities for authentic connection.

This organizational intuition allows you to contribute to group effectiveness by addressing underlying dynamics and needs rather than just surface-level problems or symptoms. You become skilled at sensing the emotional climate of groups and identifying interventions that support collective wellbeing and productivity without imposing your personal agenda on others.

Advanced intuitive leadership also involves making decisions that serve long-term collective good even when they conflict with short-term personal advantage, guided by inner wisdom that recognizes the interconnected nature of individual and community wellbeing. You might choose career directions that contribute to social healing rather than maximizing personal income, or make relationship choices that honor everyone's authentic needs rather than just your immediate preferences.

This service orientation emerges naturally from mature intuitive development because inner wisdom tends to reveal solutions that benefit everyone involved rather than creating win-lose outcomes that serve some people at the expense of others. When you consistently follow authentic inner guidance, you discover that what truly serves your highest good also serves the highest good of others, even when this isn't immediately obvious.

The advanced practice includes developing comfort with making decisions that others might not understand or approve of when your inner wisdom clearly indicates a direction that conflicts with conventional expectations or social pressure. This requires courage to follow authentic guidance even when you can't fully explain your reasoning to people who expect logical justification for every choice.

This independent decision-making doesn't mean ignoring input from others or making choices that harm people, but rather maintaining the capacity to act according to your deepest knowing even when external voices suggest different directions. You learn to receive feedback and advice while maintaining connection to your own inner authority as the final arbiter of choices that affect your life direction.

Intuitive leadership ultimately involves modeling what becomes possible when someone learns to trust the wisdom that emerges from integrated living rather than depending solely on external expertise, social approval, or conventional approaches to complex challenges. Your way of making decisions demonstrates an alternative to purely analytical or emotion-driven choice-making that inspires others to develop their own capacity for inner guidance.

This modeling influence occurs naturally through your presence and decision-making style rather than through explicit teaching, as others observe the quality of your choices and the outcomes you create through trusting inner wisdom. Your life becomes a demonstration of what becomes possible when someone learns to integrate analytical intelligence with intuitive knowing in service of authentic expression and collective wellbeing.

Creating Your G.I.F.T.S. Legacy

Creating your G.I.F.T.S. legacy involves recognizing that your personal transformation naturally generates positive influence that extends far beyond your individual life, inspiring others through authentic demonstration of what becomes possible when someone consistently applies gratitude, intuitive wisdom, meaningful relationships, applied learning, and self-compassion to their daily experience. This legacy emerges organically from integrated living rather than through conscious efforts to teach or convince others to adopt your approach.

The foundation of legacy creation lies in understanding that your way of being in the world creates ripple effects that influence everyone you encounter, from family members and close friends to casual acquaintances and strangers who observe how you handle challenges, treat other people, and respond to both positive and difficult circumstances. These influences occur through modeling rather than preaching, demonstration rather than explanation.

Your integrated G.I.F.T.S. practice creates a quality of presence that others find attractive and inspiring because it demonstrates possibilities for living that feel both authentic and sustainable rather than forced or performative. People notice when someone consistently responds to stress with grace, treats others with genuine respect and appreciation, makes decisions with confidence and wisdom, and maintains joy and resilience during challenging periods.

This attractive quality of integrated living naturally draws questions and curiosity from others who want to understand how you've developed capacities that they admire and would like to cultivate in their own lives. Your legacy begins with these informal conversations where people ask about your approach to relationships, decision-making, stress management, or personal growth because they've observed results they find impressive or inspiring.

The key to effective legacy sharing involves meeting people where they are rather than overwhelming them with complete information about all five G.I.F.T.S. key areas simultaneously. Someone who's struggling with anxiety might benefit most from learning about gratitude practices and self-compassion, while someone facing major life decisions might be most interested in developing intuitive guidance, and someone feeling isolated might need to focus on relationship presence and authenticity.

This personalized approach to sharing wisdom demonstrates respect for others' individual journeys and current capacity rather than imposing a one-size-fits-all solution that might not match their personality, circumstances, or readiness for change. You learn to sense what aspects of your experience would be most valuable for each person based on their expressed needs and interests rather than your enthusiasm for particular practices.

Legacy creation also involves sharing your struggles and failures alongside your successes and insights because authentic influence requires vulnerability that helps others recognize that transformation is possible for imperfect people rather than only for those who seem to have everything figured out. Your willingness to discuss challenges you've faced and mistakes you've made creates permission for others to begin their own growth journeys from wherever they currently are.

This honest sharing might involve discussing how you've recovered from periods when you abandoned your practices, how you've learned from relationship conflicts or poor decisions, or how you continue to work with areas where you're still developing rather than presenting yourself as someone who has mastered all aspects of personal growth. This vulnerability makes your influence more relatable and encouraging rather than intimidating or discouraging.

The legacy dimension extends beyond individual conversations to include the impact you have on families, communities, and organizations through your way of participating in group dynamics and collective decision-making.

Your integrated approach to gratitude, wisdom, relationships, learning, and self-care influences the culture of every group you participate in by modeling alternatives to reactive, critical, or superficial ways of interacting.

You might influence your family culture by consistently expressing appreciation for each person's unique contributions, by making decisions that consider everyone's wellbeing, and by treating conflicts as opportunities for deeper understanding rather than battles to be won. Your workplace culture might shift toward more collaborative and supportive dynamics because you demonstrate how to combine high performance with genuine care for colleagues' success and wellbeing.

Creating legacy through community involvement allows your G.I.F.T.S. integration to serve purposes larger than personal fulfillment by contributing to social healing, environmental protection, education, or other causes that align with your values and utilize your particular skills and resources. This service dimension emerges naturally from gratitude for what you've received and wisdom about how you can contribute most effectively to collective wellbeing.

The specific form of your community contribution matters less than the quality of presence and intention you bring to whatever service appeals to you most authentically. Whether you volunteer with children, support environmental causes, contribute to arts organizations, or serve in religious or spiritual communities, your integrated way of being influences the effectiveness and culture of whatever groups you choose to support.

Legacy creation also includes documenting your insights and experiences in ways that can benefit others who might not have direct contact with you but could learn from your journey and discoveries. This documentation might involve writing, speaking, creating art, or developing programs that share what you've learned about integrating personal development with practical living in ways that create sustainable transformation.

The key to effective documentation involves sharing principles and processes rather than prescriptive techniques, helping others understand the underlying dynamics that create lasting change rather than just providing surface-level instructions that might not work for different personalities or circumstances. Your legacy becomes most valuable when it helps others develop their own capacity for integrated living rather than creating dependency on your specific approaches.

The ultimate expression of G.I.F.T.S. legacy involves raising children, mentoring younger people, or influencing future generations through your demonstration of what becomes possible when someone commits to lifelong learning, growth, and service guided by gratitude, wisdom, authentic relationships, applied learning, and self-compassion. This intergenerational influence creates lasting positive change that extends far beyond your individual lifetime.

Whether through parenting, teaching, mentoring, or simply being a positive example in your community, your integrated living provides a template for others to follow while adapting to their own unique circumstances and calling. Your legacy becomes part of the collective wisdom that helps humanity evolve toward greater compassion, wisdom, and sustainable ways of living together on this shared planet.

Creating your G.I.F.T.S. legacy ultimately involves recognizing that your personal transformation serves purposes larger than individual fulfillment while remaining grounded in authentic expression rather than obligation or external expectations. When your growth serves others naturally through who you've become rather than what you're trying to accomplish, your influence becomes sustainable and joyful rather than depleting and burdensome.

Advanced Implementation Process

Advanced G.I.F.T.S. practice becomes available when your basic practices have become automatic responses rather than conscious efforts, creating space for deeper exploration that expands beyond personal transformation into leadership, legacy, and service. The signs of readiness include natural development of practices without conscious effort to improve them, increased comfort with uncertainty and complexity, and the attractive quality of integrated living that draws curiosity and questions from others.

Advanced gratitude evolves from personal practice to life philosophy that influences how you interpret all experiences and contribute to collective wellbeing. Intuitive leadership develops your capacity to guide major life decisions and influence others through wisdom that integrates inner knowing with practical analysis. Creating your G.I.F.T.S. legacy involves sharing your transformation through authentic demonstration and personalized wisdom sharing that meets people where they are rather than overwhelming them with complete information.

Your first implementation step is to assess your readiness for advanced practice by reflecting on whether your basic G.I.F.T.S. practices feel natural rather than effortful, whether you're experiencing expanding benefits beyond the original five key areas, and whether others are beginning to ask about your approach to life challenges because they're attracted to qualities you're embodying. Write down specific examples of how your practices have become integrated into your identity rather than remaining separate techniques you maintain through discipline.

Notice whether you feel comfortable adapting practices to new circumstances without losing confidence in their effectiveness, whether you understand underlying principles rather than just following surface-level instructions, and whether you can maintain your growth orientation during challenging periods without abandoning your foundation. These indicators suggest you're ready to explore deeper applications that build on your established integration.

Your second step is to expand your gratitude practice into a comprehensive philosophy by developing appreciation for the full spectrum of human experience, including difficult emotions and challenging circumstances that contribute to your growth and deepen your capacity for compassion. Practice finding elements worth appreciating even during periods when your overall circumstances feel overwhelming, without forcing false positivity or denying genuine difficulties.

Extend your gratitude beyond personal benefits to include appreciation for your ability to contribute positively to others and participate in the larger web of relationships that supports all life. Begin expressing gratitude for your capacity to give as well as receive, to support as well as be supported, and to encourage growth in others as well as experience your own development.

Your third step is to begin applying your intuitive guidance to major life decisions by trusting your inner wisdom for choices that significantly impact your life direction while integrating that guidance with practical analysis rather than replacing logical thinking entirely. Start with decisions that feel important but not irreversible, building confidence in your capacity to navigate uncertainty through inner knowing combined with careful consideration of practical factors.

Practice distinguishing between situations that require immediate action based on gut feelings versus those that benefit from extended reflection, developing discernment about timing that allows you to respond appropriately to different types of circumstances. Begin sharing your decision-making insights with others who ask about your approach, focusing on principles and processes rather than specific advice about their particular situations.

Your fourth step is to identify natural opportunities for sharing your G.I.F.T.S. integration through conversations, community involvement, or creative expression that emerges from your authentic interests rather than obligation to teach or convince others. Look for ways to contribute your particular skills and resources to causes that align with your values while demonstrating integrated living through your presence and participation rather than explicit instruction.

Practice meeting people where they are by sensing which aspects of your experience would be most valuable for each person based on their expressed needs and current circumstances rather than sharing everything you've learned regardless of their interest or readiness. Include your struggles and ongoing areas of development in your sharing to create permission for others to begin their growth journeys from wherever they currently are.

Your final step is to document your insights and experiences in ways that could benefit others who might not have direct contact with you, whether through writing, speaking, creating art, or developing programs that share what you've learned about sustainable transformation. Focus on principles and underlying dynamics rather than prescriptive techniques, helping others develop their own capacity for integrated living rather than creating dependency on your specific approaches.

Consider how your integrated living might influence future generations through parenting, mentoring, or community involvement that provides positive examples of what becomes possible when someone commits to lifelong growth guided by gratitude, wisdom, authentic relationships, applied learning, and self-compassion. Your legacy becomes most powerful when it serves others naturally through who you've become rather than what you're trying to accomplish, creating sustainable influence that extends far beyond your individual lifetime while remaining grounded in authentic expression and joyful service.

12

THE RIPPLE EFFECT

Let's say you've been practicing the G.I.F.T.S. method for months now, and something unexpected has started happening. Your teenager, who used to grunt responses to your questions, actually stopped scrolling through their phone yesterday to tell you about something interesting that happened at school. Your partner mentioned that you seem "different lately" in a way they can't quite put their finger on, but they like it. Your best friend asked what you've been doing because you seem more present during your conversations, more genuinely interested in their life, rather than waiting for your turn to talk.

These changes in how others respond to you didn't happen because you tried to change them or because you started giving advice about gratitude and self-compassion. They happened because transformation is inherently contagious. When you consistently show up with appreciation instead of complaint, presence instead of distraction, and self-respect instead of self-criticism, you create an emotional environment that naturally invites others to access their own capacity for these qualities.

But this ripple effect isn't always smooth or immediately positive. Some people in your life might resist the changes they see in you, feeling threatened by your growth or uncomfortable with the way your transformation highlights areas where they're not developing. Family members might make jokes about your "self-help phase" or create situations that test your commitment to your new ways of being. Friends might withdraw if your increased authenticity makes them feel exposed or inadequate by comparison.

Understanding how personal change affects relationships allows you to navigate these dynamics with wisdom and compassion, maintaining your growth while supporting others through their reactions to your transformation. This chapter will show you how to handle resistance gracefully, inspire positive change through example rather than advice, and create environments where everyone can flourish rather than just adapting to your individual development.

Changing Patterns

Every relationship operates as a dynamic system where each person's behavior influences and responds to the other person's actions, creating patterns of interaction that become comfortable and predictable even when they're not particularly healthy or satisfying. When you change how you show up in these systems through your G.I.F.T.S. practice, you inevitably disrupt established patterns and force adjustments that can feel uncomfortable or threatening to people who were invested in maintaining familiar dynamics.

Your gratitude practice changes relationships because appreciation creates emotional safety that allows others to be more vulnerable and authentic, but it also highlights the absence of appreciation in interactions where criticism and complaint have become normal. When you start expressing genuine gratitude for your partner's contributions instead of focusing on what they're not doing well, they might initially feel suspicious of your motives or uncomfortable with positive attention they're not used to receiving.

Similarly, when you begin responding to family conflicts with curiosity instead of defensiveness, asking questions to understand different per-spectives rather than immediately arguing your position, you change the entire dynamic of how disagreements unfold. Some family members might appreciate this shift toward more respectful communication, while others might feel frustrated that they can no longer engage you in the reactive patterns that used to provide them with emotional release or control.

Your developing intuitive wisdom affects relationships because trusting your inner guidance often leads to choices that prioritize authentic expression over people-pleasing, healthy boundaries over unlimited availability, and long-term relationship health over short-term harmony. When you start saying no to requests that don't align with your values or capacity, some people might feel rejected or abandoned, even when your boundaries actually create more sustainable ways of supporting them.

The increased presence you bring to relationships through your G.I.F.T.S. practice creates deeper intimacy and connection, but it also reveals superficial aspects of relationships that were previously hidden by mutual distraction and surface-level interaction. When you start showing up with genuine interest in others' inner experiences rather than just exchanging information about schedules and activities, some people might feel exposed or inadequate if they're not comfortable with emotional intimacy.

Your commitment to applying wisdom and learning from experiences changes relationships because it often leads to insights about patterns that aren't serving anyone well, even when those patterns feel familiar and safe. You might recognize that certain friendships are based primarily on complaining about life rather than supporting each other's growth, or that family gatherings consistently involve dynamics that leave everyone feeling drained rather than nourished.

Acting on these insights by suggesting different approaches or simply changing your own participation in unhealthy patterns can trigger resistance from people who benefit from the status quo or who interpret your changes as criticism of how things have always been done. Your growth can feel like implicit judgment of their choices, even when you're not trying to change anyone but yourself.

The self-compassion you develop through these G.I.F.T.S. practices affects relationships because treating yourself with kindness often reveals how harshly you and others have been treating each other through criticism, sarcasm, or emotional withdrawal during conflicts. When you stop accepting treatment that you wouldn't tolerate toward a good friend, some relationships might need to evolve significantly or end if the other person isn't willing to interact with basic respect and consideration.

Your increased self-care also changes relationship dynamics because meeting your own needs consistently means you're less likely to seek validation, entertainment, or emotional regulation from others in ways that create dependency or resentment. When you start managing your own emotional state through healthy practices rather than expecting others to keep you happy or calm, some people might feel less needed or important in your life, even though the relationship actually becomes healthier and more sustainable.

These systemic changes in how you participate in relationships create opportunities for everyone to grow and develop more authentic ways of connecting, but they also require adjustments that can feel uncomfortable or threatening during transition periods. People need time to adapt to your changes and discover how to interact with the person you're becoming rather than the person you used to be.

The key to navigating these relationship changes successfully involves maintaining compassion for others' adjustment processes while staying committed to your own growth, recognizing that temporary discomfort often precedes deeper connection and mutual respect. When you understand that resistance to your changes is normal rather than evidence that you should abandon your development, you can support others through their adaptation while protecting the positive changes you've worked hard to create.

Most importantly, understanding the systemic nature of relationship change helps you recognize that your transformation serves everyone in your life by modeling what becomes possible when someone commits to consistent growth and authentic living. Even when others initially resist your changes, your example plants seeds that can bloom later when they're ready for their own development journey.

Handling Resistance from Family and Friends

Resistance to your positive changes often emerges in subtle ways that can catch you off guard if you're expecting others to celebrate your growth and development. Family members might make jokes about your "new age" practices or express concern that you're becoming too serious or losing your sense of humor. Friends might invite you to activities that directly conflict with your self-care boundaries or express frustration when you're no longer available to participate in complaint sessions that used to bond you together.

This resistance rarely stems from genuine concern about your wellbeing but rather from unconscious discomfort with how your changes highlight areas where others feel stuck or inadequate in their own lives. When you start responding to stress with gratitude and self-compassion instead of drama and criticism, people who are still operating from reactive patterns might feel exposed or judged by comparison, even though you're not trying to make anyone feel bad about their choices.

The most effective approach to handling this resistance involves maintaining your commitment to growth while avoiding defensive explanations or attempts to convince others that your changes are valuable. When someone makes sarcastic comments about your gratitude practice, responding with detailed explanations of why appreciation is scientifically proven to improve wellbeing often escalates conflict rather than creating understanding. Instead, you can simply continue practicing gratitude without making it a topic of debate or discussion.

Gentle consistency proves more powerful than elaborate justifications because it demonstrates the value of your practices through results rather than arguments. When people observe that you're calmer during family stress, more present during conversations, and more reliable in your commitments, they begin to associate your practices with positive outcomes rather than focusing on whether they approve of your methods.

Setting boundaries around criticism of your growth practices protects your development while maintaining relationships with people who might need time to adjust to your changes. You can acknowledge others' concerns without abandoning practices that are improving your life, using responses like "I understand this seems different from how I used to handle things, and I'm finding that this approach works better for me" rather than either defending your choices extensively or changing them to avoid conflict.

These boundaries might involve redirecting conversations away from your personal development when people become critical or dismissive, choosing not to discuss your practices with people who consistently respond negatively, or simply changing the subject when others try to engage you in debates about your lifestyle changes. You can maintain loving relationships while protecting your growth from unnecessary criticism or sabotage.

When resistance comes from people whose opinions matter deeply to you, such as parents or long-term friends, the challenge becomes more complex because their approval has historically been important for your sense of security and belonging. Learning to maintain your development path even when significant people express disapproval requires developing internal validation that doesn't depend on external agreement with your choices.

This internal validation develops through recognizing the positive changes in your own life experience rather than looking to others for confirmation that your growth is valuable. When you feel calmer, more connected to your authentic self, and more capable of handling life's challenges through your G.I.F.T.S. practice, that direct experience provides more reliable validation than any external approval could offer.

Sometimes resistance appears as subtle sabotage where people create situations that make maintaining your practices more difficult or test whether you're really committed to your changes. Family members might schedule activities during times you've designated for self-care, friends might pressure you to make decisions quickly without the reflection time you've learned to value, or colleagues might increase their demands on your time and energy to see if you'll abandon your boundaries.

Recognizing these tests as normal parts of systemic change rather than personal attacks helps you respond with clarity rather than reactivity. You can maintain your practices and boundaries while understanding that others are unconsciously checking whether your changes are permanent or temporary, whether you'll revert to old patterns under pressure, or whether your growth is strong enough to withstand social challenges.

The most challenging resistance often comes from people who interpret your changes as implicit criticism of their own choices or lifestyle. When you start eating more healthfully, exercising regularly, or managing stress through self-care practices, others might feel judged for their own habits even when you never comment on what they're doing. This projected criticism can create tension that requires careful navigation to maintain relationship harmony.

Addressing this dynamic involves explicitly acknowledging that your changes are personal choices rather than recommendations for others, emphasizing that you're focused on what works for your own circumstances rather than suggesting that everyone should adopt similar practices. You might say something like "I'm finding that these approaches help me feel better, but I know everyone needs to find what works for their own situation."

When resistance becomes persistent or hostile, you might need to limit contact with people who consistently undermine your growth or create stress that makes maintaining your practices significantly more difficult. This doesn't necessarily mean ending relationships permanently, but rather protecting your development during vulnerable periods when you're still establishing new patterns that could be disrupted by excessive external pressure or criticism.

The goal of handling resistance is maintaining your growth trajectory while preserving relationships that have value beyond their current reaction to your changes. Most people who initially resist your transformation will eventually adapt and may even become curious about your approaches when they see consistent positive results over time. Patience and compassion during adjustment periods often lead to deeper relationships built on mutual respect for each person's individual growth journey.

Inspiring Change Without Being Preachy

The most powerful way to inspire positive change in others happens through authentic demonstration rather than explicit teaching, allowing people to observe the benefits of your G.I.F.T.S. practice through how you handle challenges, treat others, and navigate daily life rather than through conversations about what they should be doing differently. This modeling approach creates curiosity and interest without triggering the resistance that often emerges when people feel like they're being instructed or corrected.

Authentic demonstration means living your values consistently rather than perfectly, showing others what becomes possible when someone commits to growth while remaining honest about your own struggles and ongoing areas of development. When people see you responding to stress with gratitude instead of complaint, making decisions with confidence rather than endless analysis, and treating yourself with kindness rather than harsh criticism, they witness alternatives to their own patterns without feeling pressured to change immediately.

This modeling influence works because it provides concrete examples of different ways of being that people can observe and evaluate based on results rather than theory. When your family sees that you stay calmer during conflicts, your friends notice that you seem more content with your life, and your colleagues observe that you handle workplace challenges with unusual grace, they begin to associate your practices with outcomes they find attractive.

The key to effective modeling involves focusing on your own growth rather than trying to demonstrate anything to others, allowing the natural benefits of your practices to speak for themselves rather than consciously performing your development for external impact. When your gratitude, intuitive decision-making, relationship presence, wisdom, and self-care emerge from genuine integration rather than a desire to impress others, they create authentic influence that feels inspiring rather than manipulative.

Responding to curiosity with humility and specificity creates opportunities for meaningful sharing when others ask about your approach to challenges they're facing. Instead of launching into comprehensive explanations of the entire G.I.F.T.S. method, you can share specific practices that relate directly to their expressed concerns, meeting them where they are rather than overwhelming them with information they didn't request.

When someone asks how you stay so calm during family drama, you might share a simple technique for pausing to appreciate something beautiful before responding to conflict rather than explaining your entire gratitude practice. When a friend wonders how you make decisions with such confidence, you might describe the process of checking in with your gut feeling rather than teaching a complete course on intuitive development.

This targeted sharing demonstrates respect for others' individual journeys and current capacity rather than assuming that everyone needs the same approaches you've found helpful. Some people might be ready to explore gratitude practices but not interested in intuitive decision-making, while others might be curious about self-compassion but resistant to relationship changes that feel too vulnerable or challenging for their current circumstances.

Sharing your struggles and failures alongside your successes creates permission for others to begin their own growth journeys from wherever they currently are rather than feeling like they need to achieve your level of integration before starting. When you honestly discuss how you've recovered from periods when you abandoned your practices, learned from relationship conflicts, or worked through resistance to self-care, you normalize the imperfect process of sustainable change.

This vulnerability makes your influence more relatable and encouraging rather than intimidating or discouraging because it shows that transformation is possible for imperfect people rather than only for those who seem to have everything figured out. People need to see that growth happens through cycles of progress and setback rather than linear movement toward perfection if they're going to feel hopeful about their own capacity for positive change.

Creating environments that naturally support others' growth involves bringing your G.I.F.T.S. qualities to group situations in ways that invite similar responses without explicitly asking for them. When you express genuine appreciation for different people's contributions during family gatherings, others often begin acknowledging each other's positive qualities. When you ask thoughtful questions that show real interest in people's experiences, conversations naturally become more meaningful and connected.

This environmental influence works because it shifts group dynamics toward more positive interactions without requiring anyone to consciously adopt new practices. People tend to match the emotional tone and interaction style that others model, so your consistent presence, appreciation, and authentic interest gradually influence the overall quality of shared experiences.

Avoiding the "fix-it" mentality prevents your inspiration from becoming preachy advice-giving that creates resistance rather than openness to change. When people share problems or struggles with you, responding with empathy and questions rather than immediately offering solutions demonstrates respect for their capacity to find their own answers while creating space for them to discover insights that emerge from their own wisdom rather than your recommendations.

This supportive approach might involve reflecting back what you hear about their situation, asking questions that help them explore different perspectives, or simply providing presence and understanding that allows them to process their experience without feeling like they need to implement your suggestions or justify their choices. Sometimes people need to be heard and validated more than they need advice or solutions.

The most sustainable inspiration happens when others discover benefits of growth practices through their own experimentation rather than through compliance with your recommendations. When someone tries expressing more gratitude because they've observed how it affects your mood and relationships, they're more likely to continue the practice than if they're following your instructions about what they should do to feel better.

This self-directed discovery creates ownership and investment in positive changes rather than dependency on your guidance or approval, leading to more authentic and lasting transformation that serves their individual needs and circumstances rather than mimicking your specific approaches. Your role becomes creating conditions where others can recognize their own capacity for growth rather than teaching them how to become more like you.

Creating a G.I.F.T.S. Culture

Creating a G.I.F.T.S. culture involves gradually introducing the principles of gratitude, intuitive wisdom, authentic connection, applied learning, and self-compassion into your family and work environments through consistent modeling and gentle invitation rather than imposing new rules or expectations that might trigger resistance from people who weren't involved in choosing these approaches. This cultural shift happens organically through your influence on group dynamics and shared experiences.

Home culture transformation begins with bringing your personal G.I.F.T.S. practice into family interactions in ways that enhance everyone's experience without requiring them to adopt specific practices or change their behavior to match your development. When you consistently express appreciation for family members' contributions, respond to conflicts with curiosity rather than defensiveness, and treat yourself with kindness during stressful periods, you create an emotional environment that naturally invites similar responses from others.

Introducing gratitude into family culture might involve starting dinner conversations with each person sharing something they appreciated about their day, creating bedtime routines where everyone acknowledges something good that happened, or simply expressing more frequent and specific appreciation for family members' efforts and positive qualities. These practices work best when they feel natural and enjoyable rather than forced or obligatory.

The key to successful implementation involves making gratitude practices feel like celebrations rather than assignments, focusing on genuine appreciation that emerges from paying attention to what's actually wonderful about your shared life rather than trying to generate positive feelings about everything. Children especially respond well to gratitude practices that acknowledge their authentic experiences rather than demanding that they feel grateful for things that don't genuinely move them.

Encouraging intuitive decision-making in family culture involves creating space for everyone to check in with their feelings and preferences before making choices that affect the group, whether those decisions involve weekend activities, vacation destinations, or how to handle conflicts that arise between family members. This approach honors everyone's inner wisdom while building skills for accessing and trusting gut feelings about various options.

You might introduce family decision-making processes that include both practical considerations and intuitive responses, asking questions like "What feels right to everyone?" alongside "What makes the most sense logically?" This integration teaches family members to value both analytical thinking and inner knowing as sources of guidance for navigating choices together.

Creating authentic connection in family culture involves establishing regular opportunities for meaningful conversation that goes beyond logistics and surface-level information sharing. This might include weekly family meetings where everyone shares what's really happening in their lives, monthly one-on-one time between parents and children for deeper conversations, or simply protecting family meals from digital distractions that prevent genuine interaction.

These connection practices work best when they're adapted to your family's personality and schedule rather than following rigid formats that feel artificial or burdensome. Some families thrive with structured sharing times, while others prefer spontaneous conversations that emerge during car rides, walks, or bedtime routines. The goal is to create consistent opportunities for family members to know each other's inner experiences rather than just coordinating schedules and activities.

Workplace culture change requires more subtle approaches because you typically have less influence over organizational structures and policies, but you can still create a significant positive impact through how you participate in meetings, respond to stress, treat colleagues, and handle challenges that arise in your professional environment. Your consistent modeling of G.I.F.T.S. principles gradually influences team dynamics and collaborative relationships.

Bringing gratitude into workplace culture might involve acknowledging colleagues' contributions more frequently and specifically, expressing appreciation for teamwork and creative solutions during meetings, or simply responding to workplace challenges with perspective and resilience rather than complaint and drama. These approaches create more positive work environments without requiring organizational policy changes or formal gratitude programs.

Encouraging wisdom application in workplace culture involves sharing insights from your professional learning in ways that benefit team effectiveness, asking thoughtful questions during problem-solving discussions, and demonstrating how to learn from mistakes rather than hiding them or blaming others when things don't go perfectly. This approach creates cultures of continuous learning rather than perfectionism and defensiveness.

You might suggest brief reflection periods after completed projects, where teams discuss what worked well, what could be improved, and what insights emerged that could inform future work. These learning practices help organizations become more effective while building cultures that value growth and development rather than just immediate results and problem avoidance.

Creating self-compassion in workplace culture involves modeling how to handle mistakes and setbacks with a learning orientation rather than self-attack, setting appropriate boundaries around work demands that exceed reasonable limits, and treating colleagues with the same respect and consideration you would want during your own challenging periods. This approach reduces workplace stress while maintaining high performance standards.

You might demonstrate self-compassion by acknowledging your own mistakes honestly while focusing on solutions rather than self-criticism, asking for help when you need it rather than struggling in isolation, and taking care of your energy and wellbeing in ways that allow you to contribute sustainably to team goals rather than burning out from excessive demands.

The most effective cultural change happens gradually through consistent influence rather than dramatic interventions that might trigger resistance or skepticism from people who weren't involved in choosing new approaches. When your G.I.F.T.S. practice naturally improves your relationships, decision-making, and stress management in ways that benefit everyone around you, others become curious about your approaches rather than defensive about suggestions for change.

Measuring cultural change involves noticing shifts in group dynamics, communication patterns, and overall emotional climate rather than tracking specific behaviors or compliance with particular practices. You might observe that family conflicts resolve more quickly with less lingering resentment, that workplace meetings become more collaborative and creative, or that people in your environments seem more comfortable being authentic and vulnerable during conversations.

These cultural shifts create positive feedback loops where improved group dynamics make it easier for individuals to maintain their own growth practices while contributing to collective wellbeing, creating environments where everyone can flourish rather than just adapting to one person's individual development. When G.I.F.T.S. principles become woven into the fabric of your shared environments, they support everyone's growth and happiness rather than serving only your personal transformation.

Sharing the Implementation Process

Personal transformation inevitably affects your relationships because every relationship operates as a dynamic system where changes in one person's behavior disrupt established patterns and require adjustments from everyone involved. Your G.I.F.T.S. practice creates emotional safety and deeper connection, but it also reveals superficial aspects of relationships and can trigger resistance from people who feel threatened by your growth or uncomfortable with how your changes highlight their own areas of stagnation.

Handling resistance effectively involves maintaining your commitment to growth while avoiding defensive explanations, setting boundaries around criticism of your practices, and recognizing that temporary discomfort often precedes deeper connection and mutual respect. Inspiring change in others happens most powerfully through authentic demonstration rather than explicit teaching, allowing people to observe the benefits of your practices through results rather than arguments while sharing struggles alongside successes to normalize the imperfect process of sustainable transformation.

Your first implementation step is to prepare for relationship changes by identifying people in your life who might resist your growth and developing specific strategies for maintaining your practices while handling their reactions with compassion rather than defensiveness. Write down responses you can use when others criticize your development, such as "I understand this seems different, and I'm finding this approach works better for me," rather than elaborate justifications or abandonment of beneficial practices.

Practice setting boundaries around discussions of your personal development by redirecting conversations away from your practices when people become critical, choosing not to share details about your growth with people who consistently respond negatively, and maintaining loving relationships while protecting your development from unnecessary criticism or sabotage.

Your second step is to focus on authentic demonstration rather than conscious teaching by living your G.I.F.T.S. values consistently in your daily interactions without trying to prove anything to others or perform your development for external impact. Allow the natural benefits of your practices to speak for themselves through how you handle stress, treat others, and navigate challenges rather than discussing your methods unless others express genuine curiosity.

When people do ask about your approach to specific challenges, share targeted information that relates directly to their expressed concerns rather than overwhelming them with comprehensive explanations of your entire system. Meet them where they are by offering simple techniques that address their immediate needs while respecting their individual journey and current capacity for change.

Your third step is to begin creating G.I.F.T.S. culture in your home by introducing gratitude, authentic connection, and wisdom-sharing into family interactions through practices that feel natural and enjoyable rather than forced or obligatory. This might involve starting meals with appreciation sharing, creating regular opportunities for meaningful conversation beyond logistics, or establishing family learning discussions after significant experiences or challenges.

Adapt these cultural practices to your family's personality and schedule rather than following rigid formats, focusing on genuine experiences that enhance everyone's wellbeing rather than compliance with specific techniques. Include children's authentic preferences and responses rather than demanding that they feel grateful for things that don't genuinely move them, creating celebrations of what's actually wonderful rather than forced positivity.

Your fourth step is to influence workplace culture through subtle modeling of G.I.F.T.S. principles in your professional interactions, expressing appreciation for colleagues' contributions, responding to challenges with resilience rather than drama, and demonstrating how to learn from mistakes rather than hiding them or blaming others. These approaches gradually improve team dynamics and collaborative relationships without requiring organizational policy changes.

Suggest brief reflection periods after completed projects where teams discuss what worked well and what insights emerged for future work, creating cultures of continuous learning rather than perfectionism. Model self-compassion by handling your own mistakes with learning orientation, setting appropriate boundaries around excessive demands, and treating colleagues with respect during their challenging periods.

Your final step is to measure the ripple effects of your transformation by noticing shifts in group dynamics, communication patterns, and overall emotional climate in your family and work environments rather than tracking specific behaviors or compliance with particular practices. Look for signs that conflicts resolve more quickly with less lingering resentment, that conversations become more meaningful and connected, and that people feel more comfortable being authentic and vulnerable.

Document these positive changes in your relationships and environments to remind yourself that your personal growth serves purposes larger than individual fulfillment, creating conditions where everyone can flourish rather than just adapting to your development. Use your weekly review to assess how your G.I.F.T.S. practice is influencing others and identify opportunities to deepen your positive impact through continued authentic demonstration of integrated living that inspires others through example rather than instruction.

Remember that cultural change happens gradually through consistent influence rather than dramatic interventions, and that your patient modeling of gratitude, wisdom, connection, learning, and self-compassion plants seeds that may bloom in others when they're ready for their own growth journey. Your transformation becomes a gift not just to yourself but to everyone whose life you touch through your commitment to living from your highest and most authentic self.

13

YOUR NEW NORMAL

You stand at a threshold that most people never reach, not because they lack the capacity, but because they abandon their growth journey before arriving at this moment of profound recognition. The person looking back at you from the mirror has changed in ways that go far deeper than surface-level improvements or temporary modifications to daily routines. The gratitude that flows through your awareness feels as natural as breathing. The inner wisdom that guides your decisions has become a trusted companion rather than a distant voice you strain to hear. Your relationships pulse with authentic connection that nourishes everyone involved.

The wisdom you've gathered over months and years of learning doesn't sit idle in your mental library anymore. It lives through your choices, your responses to challenges, and your way of moving through the world with purpose and grace. Perhaps most remarkably, you treat yourself with a kindness and respect that would have felt impossible when you first began this journey, creating an internal environment where continued growth feels inevitable rather than effortful.

This transformation didn't happen through a single breakthrough moment or perfect implementation of ideal practices. It emerged through the patient, persistent application of five interconnected principles that gradually rewired your neural pathways, shifted your emotional baseline, and created new automatic responses that serve your highest good without requiring constant conscious management to maintain.

But this moment of recognition isn't an endpoint; it's a graduation into possibilities that weren't accessible when you were still learning the fundamentals. The foundation you've built through consistent G.I.F.T.S. practice now supports explorations and contributions that extend far beyond personal development into realms of service, creativity, and influence that emerge naturally from the fullness you've created rather than from obligation or external expectations.

The Person You're Becoming

The most profound shift in your G.I.F.T.S. journey happens when you realize that you're no longer someone who practices gratitude; you're someone who sees life through grateful eyes, finding genuine appreciation even in circumstances that used to trigger automatic complaint or dissatisfaction. This isn't forced positivity or denial of legitimate challenges, but rather a fundamental change in your perceptual habits that allows you to notice beauty, meaning, and opportunity in experiences that most people overlook or dismiss as ordinary.

Your grateful perspective has become so integrated into your identity that expressing appreciation feels as natural as commenting on the weather, emerging spontaneously from your authentic response to the richness and complexity of human experience rather than from conscious effort to maintain a positive attitude. People notice this quality in your presence without being able to name exactly what feels different about how you engage with life's inevitable mixture of joy and sorrow, success and disappointment, connection and solitude.

The intuitive wisdom that once felt elusive and unreliable now operates as your primary guidance system for navigating both daily decisions and major life transitions, providing clear direction that you trust even when it conflicts with conventional logic or social expectations. You've learned to distinguish between fear-based mental chatter and authentic inner knowing through years of experimentation and observation, building confidence in your capacity to access wisdom that emerges from your complete life experience rather than just your analytical thinking.

This trust in your inner guidance has transformed your relationship with uncertainty from anxiety-provoking struggle into curious exploration, allowing you to make choices and take actions based on what feels aligned with your deepest values even when you can't predict or control the outcomes. You've discovered that following authentic inner direction consistently leads to experiences that serve your growth and contribute to collective wellbeing, even when the path doesn't match your original expectations or preferences.

Your relationships have evolved from surface-level interactions focused on logistics and social obligations into soul-deep connections that provide mutual nourishment and support for everyone's authentic expression and continued development. You've learned to show up with presence that creates emotional safety for vulnerability and honest communication, while maintaining healthy boundaries that protect your energy and allow you to contribute sustainably rather than giving until you're depleted.

The quality of attention you bring to conversations and shared experiences has become a gift that others treasure because it provides the rare experience of feeling truly seen, heard, and valued for who they are rather than evaluated for how well they meet external expectations or social roles. Your capacity for authentic connection has created a network of relationships that support your continued growth while providing opportunities for service and contribution that feel meaningful rather than obligatory.

The wisdom you've accumulated through years of learning and experience now gets applied automatically to new situations rather than remaining as intellectual knowledge that you struggle to implement when facing real-world challenges. You've developed the capacity to recognize patterns, extract insights from difficulties, and adapt successful strategies to novel circumstances without having to consciously remember lessons you've learned or principles you've studied.

This integrated wisdom operates through your intuitive responses and decision-making processes rather than requiring deliberate analysis or consultation with external authorities, creating a sense of inner authority and confidence that allows you to navigate complex situations with grace and effectiveness. You've become someone who learns continuously from experience while living consistently from accumulated understanding rather than someone who collects insights without embodying them practically.

Perhaps most significantly, you've developed a relationship with yourself characterized by genuine kindness, respect, and compassion that provides an unshakeable foundation for all other aspects of your growth and contribution. The harsh internal critic that once dominated your mental landscape has been transformed into a supportive inner ally that offers honest assessment without character assassination, encouraging continued development without demanding impossible perfection.

This self-compassion has created internal conditions where taking risks, making mistakes, and facing challenges feels safe rather than threatening because you know you'll treat yourself with understanding and support regardless of outcomes. You've discovered that self-kindness actually increases motivation and resilience rather than creating complacency or lowered standards, allowing you to pursue meaningful goals with sustained energy and enthusiasm.

The person you're becoming through consistent G.I.F.T.S. practice embodies qualities that feel both completely natural and remarkably different from who you were when you began this journey. You haven't become someone else. You've become more authentically yourself, with access to capacities and ways of being that were always present but obscured by conditioning, fear, and disconnection from your deeper wisdom and inherent worth.

This authentic self-expression creates a magnetic quality that draws opportunities, relationships, and experiences that align with your values and support your continued evolution rather than requiring you to compromise your integrity or exhaust yourself trying to fit into circumstances that don't match who you've become. Your life begins to feel like a natural expression of your gifts and interests rather than a series of obligations you manage through willpower and external motivation.

Momentum for Lifelong Growth

The challenge of maintaining momentum for lifelong growth lies not in sustaining motivation or discipline, which inevitably fluctuate with changing circumstances and life seasons, but in creating systems and perspectives that support continued evolution even during periods when active personal development feels impossible or irrelevant. True momentum emerges from integrating growth orientation so deeply into your identity that learning, adapting, and expanding feel as natural as breathing rather than projects you manage through conscious effort.

Sustainable momentum requires shifting from improvement-focused thinking that seeks to fix problems or achieve specific outcomes to evolution-focused thinking that embraces change as the fundamental nature of life itself, making adaptation and development ongoing responses to an ever-changing world rather than temporary activities you engage in to reach particular destinations. This evolutionary perspective prevents the stagnation that occurs when people achieve their initial goals and then stop growing because they believe they've arrived at some final state of completion.

The key to maintaining lifelong momentum involves recognizing that each stage of development creates new capacities and interests that naturally generate curiosity about previously unexplored territories, making continued growth feel exciting rather than obligatory. When your gratitude practice has become automatic, you might become interested in how appreciation can serve community healing or environmental stewardship. When your intuitive wisdom feels reliable, you might explore how inner guidance can inform creative expression or professional leadership.

This organic expansion of interests prevents the boredom and plateau effects that cause many people to abandon personal development after achieving initial transformation, replacing the sense of having completed their growth work with recognition that each level of integration opens doorways to previously invisible possibilities for contribution and expression that couldn't be accessed from earlier stages of development.

Creating sustainable momentum also requires developing what researchers call "learning agility," the capacity to extract insights and wisdom from all experiences, whether they feel positive or challenging, successful or disappointing, expected or surprising. This learning orientation transforms every life event into potential material for continued growth rather than viewing difficulties as obstacles to development or pleasant experiences as rewards for previous effort.

You learn to ask questions like "What is this experience teaching me about myself, about life, about how I want to contribute to the world?" regardless of whether the experience matches your preferences or expectations, creating a relationship with reality that finds value and meaning in whatever emerges rather than only appreciating circumstances that feel immediately pleasant or beneficial.

Maintaining momentum through different life seasons requires adapting your growth practices to match your current capacity, circumstances, and developmental needs rather than trying to maintain identical routines regardless of changing conditions. During periods of high stress or major transitions, your practices might focus on stability and basic self-care rather than expansion and new learning. During seasons of relative calm and abundance, you might explore deeper applications or more challenging areas of development.

This adaptive flexibility prevents the all-or-nothing thinking that causes people to abandon their growth practices entirely when life becomes overwhelming or when their interests shift toward different areas of exploration. You learn to scale your practices up or down based on available energy while maintaining the core commitment to learning and evolution that keeps momentum alive even during challenging periods.

Building momentum for lifelong growth also involves creating what psychologists call "regenerative practices," activities and approaches that restore your energy and enthusiasm for continued development rather than depleting your resources through constant effort and striving. These might include time in nature that reconnects you to the larger rhythms of growth and change, creative expression that allows your insights to flow through artistic channels, or service activities that remind you how your personal development contributes to collective wellbeing.

These regenerative practices prevent the burnout that can occur when personal development becomes another form of self-improvement work rather than a natural expression of your curiosity about life and commitment to contributing your gifts to the world. When growth feels nourishing rather than effortful, maintaining momentum becomes sustainable over decades rather than just months or years.

The social dimension of sustainable momentum involves surrounding yourself with people who support and encourage continued learning rather than expecting you to remain static or comfortable with previous levels of development. This might mean cultivating friendships with others who share your commitment to growth, joining communities focused on lifelong learning, or finding mentors and teachers who can guide your exploration of new territories as your interests and capacities expand.

Creating social support for continued growth also involves learning to navigate relationships with people who prefer stability and predictability, helping them understand that your continued evolution serves everyone by making you more capable of contribution and less likely to become stagnant or resentful about unexpressed potentials that remain undeveloped due to social pressure to stop changing.

Perhaps most importantly, maintaining momentum for lifelong growth requires developing what spiritual traditions call "beginner's mind," the capacity to approach familiar practices and new experiences with fresh curiosity rather than assuming you already know everything important about areas you've been exploring for years. This openness prevents the expertise trap that causes people to stop learning when they become competent in particular areas.

Beginner's mind allows you to discover new layers and applications of basic practices you've been using for years, finding fresh insights in gratitude exercises you've done hundreds of times or noticing subtle aspects of intuitive guidance that weren't accessible when you were still learning to trust your inner wisdom. This renewable curiosity ensures that even familiar practices continue to support your growth rather than becoming routine activities you perform without engagement or discovery.

The ultimate key to lifelong momentum lies in recognizing that growth itself is not a destination you reach but a way of engaging with life that creates ongoing fulfillment and contribution regardless of external circumstances or achievements. When evolution becomes your natural response to being alive rather than a project you undertake to improve yourself, momentum becomes self-sustaining because it emerges from your fundamental orientation toward learning and service rather than depending on external motivation or specific outcomes.

Your Personal G.I.F.T.S. Mission Statement

Creating your personal G.I.F.T.S. mission statement involves distilling years of practice and integration into a clear vision of how you want to live these five principles and what kind of impact you want to have on the world, providing direction and meaning that guides your continued development while connecting your personal growth to purposes larger than individual fulfillment. This mission emerges from your authentic values and experiences rather than external expectations or generic templates that might not match your unique combination of gifts, interests, and calling.

The foundation of your mission statement lies in recognizing how your integrated G.I.F.T.S. practice has revealed your deepest values and most authentic ways of contributing to collective wellbeing, showing you what matters most when you're operating from your highest self rather than from conditioning, fear, or social pressure. These values provide the core principles that guide your decisions and shape your vision of how you want to use your remaining years on this planet.

Your gratitude practice has likely revealed what you most deeply appreciate about life. Perhaps the beauty of human connection, the wonder of natural systems, the power of creative expression, or the resilience of the human spirit in facing challenges. These appreciations point toward areas where your energy and attention naturally flow when you're not distracted by superficial concerns or obligations that don't align with your authentic interests.

Your intuitive development has probably shown you what kinds of decisions and directions feel most aligned with your deepest knowing, revealing patterns in the choices that create energy and enthusiasm versus those that feel draining or disconnected from your authentic self. This self-knowledge provides guidance about how you want to spend your time and energy in ways that honor your unique gifts and interests while serving purposes that feel meaningful rather than merely productive.

Your relationship experiences through G.I.F.T.S. practice have demonstrated what kinds of connections nourish your soul and bring out your best qualities, while also showing you how your way of being affects others and creates opportunities for mutual growth and support. This understanding of your relational gifts and needs informs your vision of how you want to contribute to community wellbeing and create environments where everyone can flourish.

The wisdom you've applied and integrated has revealed which insights and principles feel most essential for navigating life's complexities with grace and effectiveness, pointing toward the knowledge and understanding you most want to embody and share with others who might benefit from what you've learned through your journey of growth and discovery.

Your self-compassion development has shown you what you need to feel genuinely cared for and supported, while also demonstrating how treating yourself with kindness affects your capacity to show up generously for others without depleting yourself through unsustainable giving or people-pleasing that compromises your authentic expression and long-term wellbeing.

Crafting your mission statement involves weaving these insights together into a coherent vision that captures both who you want to be and how you want to contribute, creating language that inspires and guides you while remaining flexible enough to evolve as you continue growing and discovering new aspects of your potential and calling.

An effective G.I.F.T.S. mission statement typically includes several key elements that provide comprehensive guidance for living your values and maximizing your positive impact. The gratitude component might describe how you want to see and appreciate life, perhaps committing to finding beauty and meaning in all experiences while expressing appreciation in ways that help others recognize their own value and the goodness present in their circumstances.

The intuitive intention element might articulate your commitment to trusting your inner wisdom while making decisions that honor both your authentic needs and the wellbeing of others, perhaps promising to pause before major choices to sense what feels aligned with your deepest values and highest good while remaining open to guidance that emerges from sources beyond your analytical thinking.

Your relationship mission might express how you want to show up in connections with family, friends, colleagues, and community members, perhaps committing to bringing presence, appreciation, and authentic vulnerability to your interactions while maintaining healthy boundaries that allow you to contribute sustainably without sacrificing your own wellbeing or integrity.

The wisdom application component might describe how you want to learn from your experiences and share insights with others, perhaps promising to extract lessons from both successes and failures while offering what you've learned in ways that empower others to find their own answers rather than creating dependency on your guidance or approval.

Your self-care mission might articulate how you want to treat yourself and meet your own needs, perhaps committing to speaking to yourself with kindness, honoring your authentic desires and boundaries, and creating life conditions that support your continued growth and capacity for generous contribution to others.

The most powerful mission statements also include specific ways you want to use your unique combination of gifts, experiences, and resources to address problems you care about or support causes that align with your values, connecting your personal development to service that feels meaningful and sustainable rather than obligatory or overwhelming.

This service component might involve professional work that contributes to social healing, volunteer activities that support environmental protection, creative expression that inspires others, parenting or mentoring that helps younger people develop their own capacity for wisdom and compassion, or simply being a positive presence in your community that demonstrates what becomes possible when someone commits to integrated living.

Your mission statement should be written in language that moves and inspires you rather than sounding like a formal document or generic self-help affirmation, using words and phrases that capture your authentic voice and reflect your personal understanding of what matters most in life. This personal language ensures that your mission feels alive and relevant rather than abstract or disconnected from your daily experience.

The statement should also be specific enough to provide real guidance for decisions and priorities while remaining broad enough to encompass the various ways your calling might express itself as you continue growing and discovering new opportunities for contribution. This balance between specificity and flexibility allows your mission to guide you without limiting your evolution or forcing you into rigid patterns that might not serve your continued development.

Finally, your G.I.F.T.S. mission statement should be reviewed and updated regularly as you deepen your understanding of your values, expand your capacities, and discover new ways to contribute to collective wellbeing that weren't visible from earlier stages of your development. This evolutionary approach ensures that your mission remains current and inspiring rather than becoming a historical document that no longer reflects who you're becoming or how you want to serve the world.

Becoming Your Own Guide

The graduation from self-help consumer to self-guided practitioner represents one of the most significant milestones in any genuine transformation journey, marking the moment when you no longer need external authorities to tell you what you should be doing differently because you've developed reliable internal guidance that emerges from years of experimentation, observation, and integration of wisdom principles into your lived experience. This transition doesn't happen through achieving perfection but through building sufficient self-trust and inner authority to navigate life's complexities with confidence in your own judgment and decision-making capacity.

This shift from external dependence to internal authority occurs gradually as you accumulate evidence that your integrated G.I.F.T.S. practice provides reliable guidance for handling whatever challenges and opportunities emerge in your life, creating a track record of successful navigation that builds confidence in your ability to access wisdom and make choices that serve both your authentic development and the wellbeing of others who are affected by your decisions.

The end of self-help dependency doesn't mean you stop learning from books, teachers, and other sources of wisdom, but rather that you approach these resources as supplements to your own inner knowing rather than replacements for it. You become skilled at extracting what's valuable from various sources while filtering out what doesn't align with your experience or serve your current developmental needs, using external wisdom to enhance rather than override your internal guidance system.

This discriminating approach to learning prevents the information overload and decision paralysis that characterizes many people's relationship with personal development resources, allowing you to benefit from new insights and perspectives without losing connection to your own authentic understanding of what works for your unique combination of personality, circumstances, and life purpose.

Becoming your own guide also involves developing what psychologists call "meta-cognitive awareness," the capacity to observe your own thinking patterns, emotional responses, and behavioral tendencies with enough objectivity to recognize when you're operating from wisdom versus when you're reacting from conditioning, fear, or unmet needs that cloud your judgment and decision-making capacity.

This self-awareness allows you to catch yourself when you're drifting into old patterns that no longer serve you, make course corrections before small problems become major crises, and choose responses to challenging situations that align with your values rather than just providing immediate emotional relief or social approval that might compromise your long-term wellbeing or authentic expression.

The development of reliable self-guidance also requires learning to distinguish between different types of internal signals and knowing how to work with each one appropriately. You become skilled at recognizing when anxiety indicates genuine danger versus when it reflects old conditioning that needs compassionate attention rather than reactive avoidance. You learn when sadness calls for grieving and processing versus when it signals the need for life changes that would better align your circumstances with your authentic desires.

This emotional intelligence allows you to use your feelings as information rather than being controlled by them, creating space between your immediate reactions and your chosen responses that allows wisdom to inform your decisions even during emotionally charged situations that might have previously triggered automatic patterns of behavior that didn't serve your highest good.

Becoming your own guide also involves developing comfort with uncertainty and ambiguity rather than needing external authorities to provide clear answers to complex questions that don't have simple solutions. You learn to sit with not knowing while remaining open to guidance that might emerge from unexpected sources or through processes that unfold over time, rather than providing immediate clarity about what you should do next.

This tolerance for uncertainty allows you to navigate life's inevitable complexities with grace rather than anxiety, making decisions based on your best understanding of current circumstances while remaining flexible enough to adjust your approach as new information becomes available or as situations evolve in ways you couldn't have predicted or controlled.

The transition to self-guidance includes developing what spiritual traditions call "discernment," the ability to sense what's true and valuable versus what's misleading or harmful, even when the difference isn't immediately obvious through logical analysis alone. This discernment operates through your integrated intelligence that combines analytical thinking, emotional wisdom, intuitive knowing, and practical experience to evaluate options and opportunities with a sophisticated understanding that goes beyond surface-level appearances.

This discernment becomes particularly valuable when facing major life decisions or when encountering people and situations that present themselves attractively but might not actually serve your authentic development or contribute to collective wellbeing in ways that align with your values and long-term vision for how you want to live and contribute.

Perhaps most importantly, becoming your own guide involves recognizing that self-authority doesn't mean isolation or arrogance but rather taking appropriate responsibility for your choices and their consequences while remaining open to feedback, collaboration, and continued learning from others who share your commitment to wisdom and service. You become confident in your own judgment while remaining humble about the limitations of your perspective and the ongoing nature of growth and discovery.

This mature self-guidance creates what researchers call "authentic leadership" that influences others through demonstration rather than persuasion, inspiring people through your way of being rather than through your ability to convince them to adopt your approaches or perspectives. Your life becomes a teaching that shows what's possible when someone learns to trust their own deepest wisdom while remaining connected to the larger web of relationships and community that supports everyone's flourishing.

The end of self-help dependency ultimately represents the beginning of self-actualization; the ongoing process of expressing your unique gifts and contributing to collective wellbeing in ways that emerge from your authentic nature rather than from external expectations or obligations imposed by others who may not understand your particular calling or the specific ways you're meant to serve the world through your continued growth and generous contribution.

When you become your own guide, personal development transforms from a project you undertake to fix yourself into a natural expression of your curiosity about life and commitment to using your time on this planet in ways that honor both your individual authenticity and your connection to the larger community of life that includes all beings who share this remarkable journey of existence, growth, and discovery.

Your Integrated Implementation Process

Your G.I.F.T.S. future represents the natural evolution from practicing specific techniques to embodying integrated ways of being that operate automatically rather than requiring conscious management, creating a life that feels like authentic self-expression rather than disciplined self-improvement. The person you're becoming through consistent practice demonstrates gratitude, intuitive wisdom, meaningful relationships, applied learning, and self-compassion as natural responses rather than effortful behaviors, inspiring others through demonstration while contributing to collective wellbeing in ways that emerge from fullness rather than obligation.

Maintaining momentum for lifelong growth requires shifting from improvement-focused thinking to evolution-focused perspectives that embrace change as the fundamental nature of existence, creating adaptive practices that match your current capacity while building learning agility that extracts wisdom from all experiences. Your personal G.I.F.T.S. mission statement provides direction and meaning by connecting your individual development to service that addresses problems you care about using your unique combination of gifts and resources.

Your first implementation step is to create a comprehensive assessment of how your G.I.F.T.S. practice has transformed your automatic responses and daily experience by writing detailed descriptions of how you now naturally handle situations that used to trigger stress, reactivity, or self-criticism. Compare your current responses to challenges, relationships, and decisions with how you approached similar situations before beginning your G.I.F.T.S. journey, noting specific changes in your emotional baseline, decision-making confidence, and capacity for authentic connection.

Document examples of how gratitude now emerges spontaneously rather than requiring conscious effort, how your intuitive guidance operates reliably in both small and significant decisions, how your relationships have deepened through presence and authenticity, how you automatically apply wisdom from your experiences, and how you treat yourself with kindness that supports continued growth rather than demanding impossible perfection.

Your second step is to design your personal system for maintaining life-long growth momentum by identifying regenerative practices that restore your energy for continued development, creating adaptive versions of your core practices for different life seasons and circumstances, and establishing learning questions that help you extract wisdom from all experiences regardless of whether they feel immediately positive or challenging.

Develop specific approaches for high-stress periods when your capacity is limited, abundant seasons when you can explore deeper applications, and transition times when your interests and circumstances are changing rapidly. Create social support for continued growth by cultivating relationships with others who share your commitment to lifelong learning while learning to navigate connections with people who prefer stability and predictability.

Your third step is to craft your personal G.I.F.T.S. mission statement by reflecting on how your practice has revealed your deepest values, most authentic ways of contributing, and clearest vision of the impact you want to have on the world through your continued development and service. Write specific commitments for how you want to embody each of the five key areas while connecting your personal growth to meaningful contribution that uses your unique gifts and resources.

Include descriptions of how you want to see and appreciate life through gratitude, how you want to trust and follow your intuitive wisdom, how you want to show up in relationships with presence and authenticity, how you want to learn from experiences and share insights with others, and how you want to treat yourself with kindness that supports sustainable contribution. Connect these personal commitments to specific ways you want to serve causes or address problems that align with your values and calling.

Your fourth step is to establish your graduation from external self-help dependence to internal self-guidance by developing reliable methods for accessing your own wisdom, making decisions that align with your authentic values, and navigating uncertainty without needing constant external validation or instruction. Practice distinguishing between different types of internal signals and learning how to work with emotions, intuitions, and thoughts as sources of information rather than controllers of your behavior.

Create systems for evaluating new learning opportunities, relationship choices, and life directions based on your integrated understanding rather than external authorities or social expectations that might not match your unique circumstances and calling. Develop comfort with making decisions based on your best current understanding while remaining open to course corrections as new information becomes available.

Your final step is to begin living as a demonstration of integrated G.I.F.T.S. principles rather than someone who practices them, allowing your way of being to inspire others naturally through authentic expression rather than conscious teaching or advice-giving. Document the ripple effects of your transformation on family members, friends, colleagues, and community members who observe your approach to challenges, relationships, and daily life.

Track how your integrated living influences others to become curious about their own capacity for growth and contribution, noting opportunities to share your experience in ways that empower others to find their own answers rather than creating dependency on your guidance. Use your weekly review to assess how your personal development is serving purposes larger than individual fulfillment while ensuring that your contribution feels sustainable and joyful rather than depleting or obligatory.

Your G.I.F.T.S. future represents not an endpoint but a graduation into possibilities that emerge. The life you keep glimpsing becomes your lived reality when gratitude, intuitive wisdom, authentic relationships, applied learning, and self-compassion operate as integrated expressions of who you are rather than techniques you use to improve who you think you should become.

14

LASTING CHANGE

The book you've just completed reading represents far more than another collection of personal development strategies or motivational concepts designed to inspire temporary enthusiasm before fading into the background noise of good intentions that never quite translate into lasting change. What you hold in your hands is a systematic approach to transformation that addresses the fundamental gap between knowing what would improve your life and actually living that way consistently, day after day, year after year, until new ways of being become as natural as breathing.

The G.I.F.T.S. method succeeds where other approaches fail because it treats transformation as an integrated system rather than a collection of separate improvement projects, recognizing that gratitude, intuitive intention, family and friends connection, treasured wisdom, and self-love and care naturally reinforce each other when developed simultaneously. This interconnected approach creates upward spirals where progress in any area automatically supports progress in all others, making sustainable change feel inevitable rather than effortful.

The Simple Truth About Lasting Change

The simple truth about lasting change is that it doesn't require perfection, dramatic overhauls, or superhuman discipline, but rather the consistent practice of five interconnected areas that naturally support each other when approached as expressions of a single way of being rather than separate techniques to be managed through willpower. Your transformation happens through small, daily choices that gradually rewire your neural pathways and shift your emotional baseline until what once required conscious effort becomes automatic response.

This truth contradicts everything you've been taught about change requiring massive action, perfect consistency, or complete lifestyle overhauls that demand enormous amounts of energy and motivation to maintain. The reality is that sustainable transformation emerges through what researchers call "minimum effective dose," the smallest amount of consistent action that creates meaningful results without overwhelming your capacity or competing with other important areas of your life.

Your gratitude practice doesn't need to involve elaborate journaling rituals or forced appreciation for circumstances that genuinely feel challenging. It develops through brief moments of noticing and acknowledging what's actually working in your immediate experience, building a foundation of appreciation that gradually shifts your perceptual habits from automatic complaint toward natural recognition of beauty, meaning, and opportunity that exists in ordinary moments.

Your intuitive development doesn't require hours of meditation or mystical experiences that provide dramatic revelations about your life direction. It grows through simple practices of pausing before decisions to check in with your gut feelings, building trust in your inner wisdom through successful application to small choices before expanding to more significant life directions that benefit from the integration of analytical thinking and deeper knowing.

Your relationship connections don't need complete communication overhauls or therapy-level processing of every interaction. They deepen through presence practices that eliminate distractions during conversations, specific appreciation that helps others feel seen and valued, and authentic sharing that creates emotional safety for vulnerability and mutual understanding to develop naturally over time.

Your wisdom application doesn't require reading dozens of books or attending expensive workshops to collect more information about how you should be living. It happens through systematic capture and implementation of insights you're already receiving from your daily experiences, focusing on depth of integration rather than breadth of knowledge accumulation that often prevents rather than supports practical application.

Your self-love and care don't need elaborate wellness routines or expensive self-care products that promise to make you feel better about yourself. They develop through simple practices of speaking to yourself with the same kindness you would show a good friend, meeting your basic needs consistently, and treating your mistakes and imperfections as normal parts of the human learning process rather than evidence of personal inadequacy.

The simple truth is that when these five key areas operate together as an integrated approach to living, they create compound benefits that extend far beyond the sum of their individual effects. Your gratitude enhances your capacity for clear intuitive guidance, which leads to better relationship decisions, which creates emotional safety for applying wisdom and treating yourself with care, which supports deeper appreciation for your life experience and continued growth.

This integration creates what systems theorists call "emergent properties," qualities and capacities that arise from the interaction of elements rather than existing in any single component. The peace, joy, confidence, and resilience that emerge from consistent G.I.F.T.S. practice feel effortless to maintain because they're supported by multiple reinforcing systems rather than depending on any single technique or approach that could fail under pressure.

The simple truth about lasting change is that it becomes automatic when it aligns with your authentic nature rather than fighting against it, when it enhances your relationships rather than competing with them, and when it serves purposes larger than personal improvement by contributing to collective wellbeing in ways that feel meaningful rather than obligatory. Your transformation serves not just your individual fulfillment but the flourishing of everyone whose life you touch through your commitment to living from your highest and most integrated self.

Your Moment of Choice

This moment represents a crossroads that appears in every person's life multiple times, though most people don't recognize it as the pivotal choice point it actually is. You can close this book and return to the familiar patterns that brought you to seek transformation in the first place, treating what you've learned as interesting information that joins the mental library of good ideas you don't actually implement. Or you can recognize this as your opportunity to finally bridge the knowing-doing gap that has frustrated your previous attempts at lasting positive change.

The choice you make in the next few minutes will determine whether you become someone who consistently applies wisdom to create the warm, connected, authentic life you keep glimpsing in your moments of clarity, or whether you remain someone who knows what would improve your experience but continues operating from automatic patterns that don't serve your highest good or deepest values. This isn't a choice you can postpone until conditions are perfect or motivation feels stronger. It's a choice that must be made now, with whatever energy and circumstances you currently have available.

The gap between knowing and doing exists not because you lack intelligence, willpower, or genuine desire for positive change, but because you've been approaching transformation as a collection of separate improvement projects rather than an integrated system that leverages the natural connections between different areas of your life. Every previous attempt to change probably focused on one area at a time, requiring enormous amounts of conscious effort that inevitably got overwhelmed by other life demands and competing priorities.

The G.I.F.T.S. method bridges this gap by working with your psychology rather than against it, creating changes that feel natural rather than forced because they emerge from who you're becoming rather than being imposed from outside through discipline and willpower that inevitably get depleted by stress, fatigue, and the countless other demands on your attention and energy that characterize modern life.

Your moment of choice involves recognizing that you already have everything you need to begin immediately. You don't need more information, better circumstances, additional motivation, or permission from anyone else to start practicing gratitude during the transition moments that already exist in your daily routine. You don't need special training or ideal conditions to begin checking in with your intuition before making small decisions that provide practice for trusting your inner wisdom.

You don't need relationship expertise or communication training to start bringing more presence to conversations with people you care about, expressing specific appreciation for their contributions to your life, or sharing your authentic thoughts and feelings in ways that create opportunities for deeper connection. You don't need advanced degrees or extensive research to begin capturing insights from your daily experiences and identifying specific ways to apply what you're learning to improve how you handle similar situations in the future.

You don't need expensive wellness programs or elaborate self-care routines to begin treating yourself with basic kindness, speaking to yourself the way you would speak to someone you love, and meeting your fundamental needs for rest, nourishment, and emotional support in ways that create sustainable capacity for contributing generously to others without depleting yourself through constant giving that ignores your own wellbeing.

The choice to bridge the gap requires accepting that your transformation will happen imperfectly, gradually, and with inevitable setbacks that are part of any genuine change process rather than evidence of personal failure or inadequate commitment to growth. You must choose to begin with whatever capacity you currently have rather than waiting until you feel ready, motivated, or confident enough to implement everything perfectly from the start.

This choice also involves releasing the fantasy that lasting change happens through dramatic breakthroughs or life-altering realizations that suddenly make everything different without requiring the patient, persistent application of wisdom principles to your daily experience over months and years of gradual integration that eventually creates the automatic responses you're seeking.

Your moment of choice includes deciding whether you're willing to prioritize your own transformation enough to protect it from the countless distractions, obligations, and other people's agendas that will compete for your attention and energy if you don't create clear boundaries around what matters most for your continued development and authentic expression.

The choice involves committing to your growth even when others don't understand or support your changes, when old patterns feel more comfortable than new approaches, and when progress feels slow or invisible compared to the dramatic transformations you might have imagined when you first began seeking positive change in your life.

Most importantly, your moment of choice requires deciding whether you're ready to stop being a collector of good ideas and become someone who actually lives them, using the systematic approach you've learned to finally close the knowing-doing gap and create the integrated, authentic, meaningful life that represents your highest potential and greatest contribution to the world.

The choice is yours, and it must be made now. Will you finally bridge the gap between who you know you could be and who you actually are on a Tuesday afternoon when no one is watching and life feels ordinary rather than inspiring? Will you choose the path of consistent, imperfect, gradual transformation that leads to sustainable change, or will you return to the familiar cycle of inspiration without implementation that has characterized your previous attempts at personal development?

Your future self is waiting for your decision, and the people whose lives you'll touch through your transformation are depending on you to choose growth over comfort, integration over information, and authentic living over the safe but unsatisfying patterns that have kept you stuck in the knowing-doing gap that brought you to this book in the first place.

Your G.I.F.T.S. Action Plan

Your transformation begins not tomorrow when conditions might be more favorable, not next week when your schedule clears up, and not next month when you feel more motivated, but right now with the first small action you take to implement what you've learned before the inspiration fades and this book becomes another good idea that never quite translated into the lived reality of positive change. The next 30 days represent your bridge from understanding to embodiment, from knowing to being, from hope to actual experience of the integrated life you've been seeking.

Your action plan starts with your strongest G.I.F.T.S. area because building on existing strengths creates momentum more effectively than trying to fix your weakest areas first, allowing you to experience early success that provides motivation and confidence for addressing more challenging aspects of your development. If gratitude feels most natural, begin there and let your appreciation practice open your heart to clearer intuitive guidance. If relationships are your strength, use your connection skills as the foundation for deeper wisdom and self-care.

Your daily check-in system becomes operational immediately using the simple five-question format that takes less than sixty seconds each evening but provides the accountability and tracking that transforms good intentions into consistent actions.

Did you practice gratitude today?

Did you check in with your intuition before at least one decision?

Did you have a meaningful connection with someone you care about?

Did you capture or apply wisdom?

Did you do something that demonstrated care for yourself?

These yes-or-no questions focus on completion rather than quality, giving you credit for any engagement with each area regardless of how inspired, successful, or transformative the experience felt. On days when your practices feel forced or artificial, you still get credit for doing them because consistency builds the neural pathways that eventually make these responses feel natural rather than effortful.

Your 24-hour recovery rule becomes your safety net for the inevitable days when you drift away from your practices, providing immediate action steps that get you back on track before temporary lapses become permanent abandonment of your growth efforts. The moment you notice you've been off track, you take one small action in each G.I.F.T.S. area within twenty-four hours, regardless of how unmotivated or resistant you feel about resuming your development work.

These recovery actions should be so simple that you can complete them even when you're busy, stressed, or doubting the value of the entire approach. Appreciate three things you can see from wherever you're sitting, ask your gut feeling about what to do next, send a brief message to someone you care about, write down one thing you learned recently, and take three conscious breaths as an act of self-compassion.

Your integration practice weaves all five key areas together through daily routines that address multiple G.I.F.T.S. simultaneously rather than treating them as separate activities that compete for your limited time and attention. Your morning routine might include gratitude for the day ahead, an intuitive check-in about your priorities, appreciation for people you'll interact with, the intention to apply wisdom you've been learning, and self-care that ensures you start from a place of fullness rather than depletion.

Your weekly review becomes your navigation system for staying on course while making adjustments based on what you're learning about your patterns, preferences, and the specific approaches that work best for your personality and circumstances.

What worked well this week in each area?

What challenges did you encounter and how did you handle them?

What do you want to adjust for next week based on your experience?

This review prevents the drift that causes most people to gradually abandon their practices without noticing until they're completely off track, providing regular opportunities to celebrate progress while making course corrections that keep you moving toward the integrated life you're creating through consistent application of wisdom principles to your daily experience.

Your support system activates immediately through sharing your 30-day commitment with at least one person who cares about your wellbeing and will check in on your progress, providing external accountability that supplements your internal motivation when enthusiasm naturally fluctuates with changing circumstances and competing demands on your attention and energy.

This support doesn't require finding someone who shares your specific approach to personal development, but simply someone who wants you to succeed and will ask how you're doing with your growth practices when you see them regularly. Their interest creates gentle pressure that helps you maintain consistency even when you don't feel like continuing your practices.

Your environment preparation removes obstacles and creates cues that make positive choices easier than negative ones, leveraging the power of environmental design to support your transformation rather than relying entirely on willpower and motivation that inevitably fluctuate with your energy levels and external pressures. Put your journal next to your coffee maker, set phone reminders for intuitive check-ins, schedule relationship time like any other important appointment.

Your crisis adaptation plan prepares you for the high-stress periods, travel, illness, and other disruptions that will test your commitment to growth by having simplified versions of all practices that can be maintained regardless of circumstances. These backup approaches ensure continuity even when your normal routines become impossible, preventing the complete breaks that often lead to permanent abandonment of beneficial practices.

Your next 30 days begin with the first action you take right now, before you close this book and return to the routines and distractions that will compete for your attention if you don't immediately begin implementing what you've learned. Choose one simple action from any G.I.F.T.S. area and complete it within the next five minutes, creating momentum that carries you into the systematic practice that will gradually transform your automatic responses and daily experience.

Appreciate something beautiful you can see from where you're sitting, ask your intuition what it wants you to know about beginning this transformation journey, think of someone you care about and send them appreciation either mentally or through a brief message, identify one insight from this book that you can apply immediately, or do something kind for yourself that demonstrates the self-care that will support your continued growth and contribution to others.

Your G.I.F.T.S. future starts now, not with perfect implementation or dramatic changes, but with the first small step that begins the gradual process of becoming someone who naturally lives from gratitude, trusts inner wisdom, creates authentic connections, applies accumulated learning, and treats themselves with the compassion that makes sustainable transformation possible. The life you keep glimpsing in your moments of clarity becomes your lived reality through the consistent, imperfect, patient application of these five principles that work together to create the integrated person you're meant to become.

Remember that becoming automatic in these five key areas is how you finally become the person you've always known you could be, not through force or perfection but through the gentle persistence that allows new ways of being to emerge naturally from consistent practice that honors both your individual authenticity and your connection to the larger community of life that supports everyone's flourishing and continued growth toward their highest potential and greatest contribution to collective wellbeing.

G.I.F.T.S. Daily Practice Guide

<u>Gratitude</u>

Question: Did I practice gratitude today?

Choose ONE practice per day:

- **Transition Moments**: Pause for 10-15 seconds during coffee, hand-washing, or getting in your car. Notice one sensory detail to appreciate.
- **Express Appreciation**: Tell someone what you value about them (be specific).
- **Routine Gratitude**: Appreciate one thing you do regularly (like having clean water or a warm bed).
- **Stress Practice**: When stressed, appreciate something small and immediate (the chair you're sitting in, a deep breath).

<u>Intuitive Intention</u>

Question: Did I check in with my intuition before at least one decision today?

Choose ONE practice per day:

- **Decision Pause**: Before one choice today, pause 10 seconds and ask, "What feels right here?"
- **Morning Check-In**: Spend 3-5 minutes asking what your inner wisdom wants you to know about today.
- **Body Awareness**: Notice once today—are you tense or relaxed? What is your body telling you?

- **Intuitive Action**: Follow one small gut feeling (take a different route, call someone who's on your mind).
- **Evening Reflection**: Ask, "When did I trust my gut today?"

Family & Friends

Question: Did I have a meaningful connection with someone I care about today?

Choose ONE practice per day:

- **Present Conversation**: Give someone your full attention for 5 minutes (no phone, no distractions).
- **Reflect Back**: In one conversation, say "It sounds like you're feeling..." to show you're listening.
- **Specific Appreciation**: Tell someone one specific thing you appreciate about them.
- **Weekly Tradition**: Start one simple routine (Sunday phone call, Friday dinner, sharing daily highlights).
- **Relationship Generosity**: Do one small thoughtful act for someone you love.

Treasured Wisdom

Question: Did I capture or apply wisdom today?

Choose ONE practice per day:

- **Capture One Insight**: Write down one thing you learned or noticed today.
- **Apply One Principle**: Use one piece of wisdom you already know in a situation today.
- **Weekly Review**: Spend 5 minutes noticing which insights you're living vs. just knowing.
- **Share Wisdom**: When appropriate, share something you've learned

with someone who might benefit.
- **Audit Your Learning**: Look at your notes once a week—pick one insight to focus on this week.

Self-Love & Care

Question: Did I do something that demonstrated care for myself today?

Choose ONE practice per day:

- **Kind Self-Talk**: When you catch self-criticism, ask "How would I talk to a friend?" Then talk to yourself that way.
- **Body Check-In**: Notice how one activity makes you feel (energized or drained). Do more of what restores you.
- **Self-Compassion Moment**: Place hand on heart and say, "This is hard, and it's okay that I'm struggling."
- **Use a Supportive Phrase**: Pick one from your list like "I'm learning and mistakes are part of growth."
- **Meet One Need**: Do one thing your body/mind needs today (rest, water, movement, a break).

Weekly Review

- What worked well this week in each area?
- What challenged me?
- What will I adjust next week?

Remember:

This is a system
✓ Pick ONE practice from each area daily
✓ Answer yes if you did ANYTHING, even if imperfect
✓ If you miss a day, use the 24-hour one tiny action recovery rule
✓ Progress over perfection

G.I.F.T.S. System Guide

The G.I.F.T.S. Method consists of five key areas of your life.

The five key areas are:

Gratitude: Appreciate 3 things during transition moments

Intuitive Intention: Pause before making decisions to check your gut

Family and Friends Connection: Have a meaningful interaction, staying present

Treasured Wisdom: Capture an insight and identify how to apply it in the next 24 hours

Self-Love and Care: Do a kind thing for yourself

The practice is simply to make contact with each of the five key areas daily. If you miss a day, use the 24-Hour Recovery Rule.

Ultimate Goal: To Create an Upward Spiral: Gratitude → clearer intuition → better relationship choices → more wisdom application → deeper self-care → more gratitude

Getting Started Checklist

Before Day 1:

- Choose your start date (write it down)
- Write the five evening review questions in a notebook

Did I practice gratitude today?

Did I check in with my intuition before at least one decision?

Did I have a meaningful connection with someone I care about

Did I capture or apply wisdom?

Did I do something that demonstrated care for myself?

- Choose your evening review time (Same time every day)
- Kept track of your progress on a calendar (optional)
- Tell one supportive person about your challenge

Remember to:

- Refer to the Daily Guide for examples
- Incorporate existing routines within your practice
- Create backup plans for travel/stress/illness

Keep in mind that this is a system
- ✓ Consistency beats perfection
- ✓ Lapses are normal—recovery is the skill
- ✓ Give yourself credit for ANY engagement, even if imperfect
- ✓ This is an experiment, not a test
- ✓ By day 21-25, it starts feeling automatic
- ✓ Small daily actions = massive monthly results

30 Day Weekly Focus

WEEK ONE: Foundation

Focus: Establish basic contact with all five areas daily.
Goal: Consistency, not perfection.

- **Gratitude**: Appreciate 3 things during transition moments (coffee, car, handwashing)
- **Intuitive Intention**: Pause before ONE decision to check your gut
- **Family and Friends**: Have ONE meaningful interaction (present conversation, specific appreciation, or genuine curiosity)
- **Treasured Wisdom**: Capture ONE insight and identify how to apply it in the next 24 hours

- **Self-Love and Care**: Do ONE kind thing for yourself

Evening Review Questions (Same time every day)

1. *Answer YES or NO to the 5 questions*
   Did I practice gratitude today?
   Did I check in with my intuition before at least one decision?
   Did I have a meaningful connection with someone I care about
   Did I capture or apply wisdom?
   Did I do something that demonstrated care for myself?
2. **Celebrate**: 3+ YES answers = successful day!

Weekly Review Questions
Each Sunday ask yourself:

1. **What worked well this week in each area?**
2. **What challenged me?**
3. **What patterns do I notice in my tracking?**
4. **What will I adjust next week?**

WEEK TWO: Deepen Your Practice
Focus: Expand practices while maintaining the basic structure.
Goal: Notice how practices start supporting each other naturally.

- **Gratitude**: Add appreciation for one challenge or difficulty (find the growth opportunity)
- **Intuitive Intention**: Check in with yourself before making THREE decisions (small to medium choices)
- **Family and Friends**: Practice full presence in one conversation (no phone, no multitasking)
- **Treasured Wisdom**: Review week one insights—which did you actually use?
- **Self-Love and Care**: Notice your self-talk. Choose kinder words when

you catch criticism.

Evening Review

1. ***Answer YES or NO to the 5 questions***
   Did I practice gratitude today?
   Did I check in with my intuition before at least one decision?
   Did I have a meaningful connection with someone I care about
   Did I capture or apply wisdom?
   Did I do something that demonstrated care for myself?
2. **Celebrate**: 3+ YES answers = successful day!

Weekly Review

Notice improvements, consistency streaks, and natural integration.

1. **What worked well this week in each area?**
2. **What challenged me?**
3. **What patterns do I notice in my tracking?**
4. **What will I adjust next week?**

WEEK THREE: Integration

Focus: Observe the organic connections.
Goal: Let practices connect without forcing them.

- Notice when your gratitude includes appreciation for your intuition, relationships, and growth
- Notice when your decisions automatically consider how they affect people you love
- Notice when your interations with others start to naturally include gratitude and wisdom
- Treat lapses as information, not failure. Notice when self-compassion extends to imperfect practice (missed days are just data)

Evening Review

1. *Answer YES or NO to the 5 questions*
   Did I practice gratitude today?
   Did I check in with my intuition before at least one decision?
   Did I have a meaningful connection with someone I care about
   Did I capture or apply wisdom?
   Did I do something that demonstrated care for myself?
2. **Celebrate**: 3+ YES answers = successful day!

Weekly Review

Notice improvements, consistency streaks, and natural integration.

1. **What worked well this week in each area?**
2. **What challenged me?**
3. **What patterns do I notice in my tracking?**
4. **What will I adjust next week?**

WEEK FOUR: Momentum

Focus: Identify which practices feel most natural and which areas need more attention

Goal: Practices feel more automatic without needing to check the list

Experience the compound benefits:

- Gratitude → clearer intuition → better relationship choices → more applied wisdom → deeper self-care → more gratitude (upward spiral!)

Evening Review

1. *Answer YES or NO to the 5 questions*
   Did I practice gratitude today?
   Did I check in with my intuition before at least one decision?
   Did I have a meaningful connection with someone I care about

Did I capture or apply wisdom?

Did I do something that demonstrated care for myself?

2. **Celebrate**: 3+ YES answers = successful day!

Weekly Review

Notice improvements, consistency streaks, and natural integration.

1. **What worked well this week in each area?**
2. **What challenged me?**
3. **What patterns do I notice in my tracking?**
4. **What will I adjust next week?**

Common Resistance & Quick Fixes

When You Miss Days (24-Hour Recovery Rule)

The moment you notice you're off track, do these 5 micro-actions: *No starting over, no self-criticism.*

1. Appreciate 3 things you can see right now
2. Ask your gut: "What do I need next?"
3. Send a brief message to someone you care about
4. Write down 1 thing you learned recently
5. Take 3 conscious breaths

Loss of Motivation (Usually around days 10-15)

Solution: Make practices SMALLER, not bigger

- Gratitude = notice 1 thing
- Intuition = check in about lunch
- Connection = 2-minute text
- Wisdom = write 1 sentence

- Self-care = drink water mindfully

Perfectionism

Solution: "Imperfect practice counts fully." Forced gratitude = still gratitude

Social Skepticism

Solution: Keep practicing. Don't defend or explain. Your results will speak.

"No Time"

Solution: These practices take under 10 minutes and fit into what you're already doing.

Overwhelm

Solution: Pick just 3 areas this week. Add the others when ready.

Modified Versions for Hard Times:

- Travel: 1-minute versions of each practice
- Illness: Just do the daily check-in, give yourself credit for awareness
- Crisis: Focus only on self-care and gratitude for small things

Beyond Day 30

By the end, you'll:

- Answer "yes" to most questions without thinking
- Have practices that feel like "just who you are"
- Know which areas need continued focus
- Have a system for lifelong growth

Next Steps:

- Simplify tracking (weekly instead of daily)
- Deepen one area you love
- Teach what you've learned to someone else
- Keep going—this is just the beginning

G.I.F.T.S. Summary & Reference Guide

Lasting change happens when you consistently practice five interconnected areas that naturally support each other, transforming who you are rather than just what you do. The system works because it addresses the fundamental knowing-doing gap through integration, not information.

The Stack of Good Intentions

- The knowing-doing gap exists not from lack of information, but from missing systems for consistent application
- Most personal development fails because it treats change as separate improvements rather than an integrated system
- The G.I.F.T.S. method works because all five areas (Gratitude, Intuitive Intention, Family & Friends, Treasured Wisdom, Self-Love & Care) naturally reinforce each other
- The mindset you bring to your growth, such as, "Attitude is so important," determines whether practices take root

The Knowing-Doing Gap

- Intelligence makes the gap worse, not better - smart people analyze instead of act
- Willpower always fails because it's a limited resource that gets depleted
- The hidden cost: each failed attempt erodes self-trust and creates cynicism
- Integration principle: working on all five areas simultaneously is easier than one at a time

- Identity-based change (becoming vs. doing) creates sustainable transformation

The Integrated G.I.F.T.S. Method

- Five key areas control your daily experience: Gratitude, Intuitive Intention, Family & Friends, Treasured Wisdom, Self-Love & Care
- The interconnection effect: progress in any area automatically supports progress in others
- Implementation infrastructure: structural support + psychological protocols + recovery systems
- Personal assessment reveals your anchor area (strength) and priority area (needs work)
- Success = speed of recovery from lapses, not perfect consistency

G is for Gratitude

- Traditional gratitude practices fail because they're mental exercises, not emotional experiences
- The integration method: weave appreciation into existing transition moments (15 seconds, 3x daily)
- Gratitude becomes your relationship superpower - specific appreciation creates deeper connection
- Momentum effect: consistent gratitude naturally enhances intuition and self-compassion
- Focus on concrete, sensory experiences rather than abstract blessings

I is for Intuitive Intention

- You're disconnected from intuition due to years of being rewarded for analysis over gut feelings
- Physical sensations, emotional responses, and sudden knowing are your intuitive signals

- Effective intentions emerge from authentic desires (soul-level) not external expectations (ego-level)
- Daily practice: pause before decisions to ask "What feels right here?"
- Integration happens when checking intuition becomes as automatic as looking both ways before crossing

F is for Family and Friends

- The connection crisis: surface-level interactions that maintain appearance but leave everyone lonely
- Presence practice: eliminate distractions, bring complete attention, reflect back what you hear
- Healing distant relationships: start with appreciation, gentle curiosity, and shared positive experiences
- Create simple traditions that build on existing routines (not elaborate new obligations)
- Meaningful connection = quality of attention, not quantity of time

T is for Treasured Wisdom

- The consumption pattern: accumulating insights without application is sophisticated procrastination
- Wisdom integration process: conscious selection → experimentation → reflection → integration → embodiment
- Core life principles: 3-5 fundamental truths that guide your decisions and define your character
- Teaching test: sharing wisdom with others solidifies your own integration
- Focus on depth (embodying few principles) over breadth (collecting many insights)

S is for Self-Love and Care

- Self-criticism keeps you stuck by creating stress that clouds thinking and drains energy
- Rewrite internal dialogue: speak to yourself like you would a beloved friend
- Authentic self-care addresses deeper needs for restoration, not just temporary pleasure
- Self-compassion: recognize suffering is universal, speak kindly to yourself, meet your needs
- Self-care isn't selfish - it's the foundation that makes sustainable contribution possible

30-Day G.I.F.T.S. Integration System

- 30 days provides optimal window for establishing neural pathways without overwhelm
- Week 1: Basic contact with all five areas (<10 min/day)
- Week 2: Deepen practices while maintaining structure
- Week 3: Practices begin connecting naturally
- Week 4: Experience compound benefits and momentum
- Daily check-in: 5 yes/no questions focusing on completion, not quality

When Life Gets Messy

- Perfectionism kills transformation by creating impossible standards and all-or-nothing thinking
- 24-hour recovery rule: take one small action in each area within 24 hours of noticing drift
- Crisis adaptation: simplified versions maintain continuity when normal routines are impossible
- Setbacks contain valuable information about patterns, triggers, and needs

- Recovery speed matters more than avoiding lapses

Deepening Your Practice

- Ready for advanced practice when: practices feel automatic, others notice your qualities, you're comfortable with uncertainty
- Advanced gratitude: becomes life philosophy that influences all interpretations and contributions
- Intuitive leadership: guide major decisions and influence others through integrated wisdom
- Create your legacy: impact emerges through authentic demonstration, not preaching
- Share struggles alongside successes to normalize the imperfect process

The Ripple Effect

- Your transformation changes relationship patterns - some will resist, some will be inspired
- Handle resistance with gentle consistency, not defensive explanations or abandonment
- Inspire through demonstration: let results speak for themselves
- Create G.I.F.T.S. culture in home/work by modeling principles consistently
- Cultural change happens gradually through influence, not dramatic interventions

Your New Normal

- You're no longer someone who practices gratitude - you're someone who sees through grateful eyes
- Intuitive wisdom operates as your primary guidance system
- Relationships are soul-deep connections that nourish everyone involved
- Wisdom gets applied automatically without conscious effort

- Self-compassion provides unshakeable foundation for continued growth

Lasting Change

- Simple truth: transformation doesn't require perfection, just consistent practice of five interconnected areas
- Your moment of choice: bridge the knowing-doing gap now with whatever capacity you have
- Action plan: start with strongest area, use daily check-in system, implement 24-hour recovery rule
- Integration practice weaves all five areas into daily routines
- The life you keep glimpsing becomes your lived reality through patient, persistent application

About the Author

Elaine Lombardi, CHHC, AADP, is a Certified Holistic Health Coach and Belief Coding® facilitator dedicated to helping women navigate life transitions with compassion, clarity, and purpose. She is the author of several self-help and wellness titles, including Hurricane Lucy: A Caregiver's Guide and G.I.F.T.S. A Voyage Home to Yourself: The Keys to Unlocking Your True Light and Purpose.

With extensive experience as a teacher and director of education, Elaine brings a wealth of understanding about growth, change, and nurturing transformation. She graduated from the Institute for Integrative Nutrition in New York City and holds board certification from the American Academy of Drugless Practitioners.

Married for over fifty years, Elaine is a mother of four, a grandmother of ten, and a great-grandmother of two. When she isn't writing, she enjoys traveling and painting. Her passion is supporting women on their journeys to reclaim their authentic selves.

Connect with Elaine at ElaineLombardi.com to learn more about her work and upcoming projects.